LETTERS FROM THE SLIPPERY SLOPE

A Life-Long Creationist Tries to Make Sense of Evolution.

What Could Go Wrong?

CALVIN WRAY

Cover design by Juice Creative
Edited by Elizabeth Jones

For Dad, who has always been more comfortable with complicated questions than easy answers.

CONTENTS

PREFACE

What on God's green earth qualifies me to tackle a subject as complex and emotionally charged as the debate that routinely pits Evangelical Christians—"Bible Believers"—against several generations of science professionals? The creation/evolution conflict (and a conflict it is, in word, spit and spirit, as the legal proceedings can attest to) is rather heady stuff isn't it?

Perhaps if I had completed my degree in biology, I could bring a passionate defense of my science to the fray. But I am not a biologist. If I were a teacher, I could share tales of the red-faced anti-creationist academic scowling across the expanse of the college lecture theatre as he attempts to shred the fragile faith of the timid creationist who stood and asked a simple question about "transitional forms in the fossil record." But I'm not a teacher, and have a somewhat turbulent history with some members of that profession.

I'm not a botanist. I don't cross-pollinate nasturtiums with emerald cedars for fun or profit. I hate weeding. I recently tore up our front lawn and put down rocks in an attempt to lower the mortality rate of beings under my care. I am not a chemist. I still smirk when I hear someone use the term "inert gas" and until recently, I was convinced "nuclear winter" was a breath mint.

My official rank as outsider, however, which separates me from the roster of the learned and lettered, is precisely why I believe I may be the most qualified person ever to write on this subject. I don't have any skin in the game! My total lack of vocational expertise in either the sciences or theology has prepared me to take on the role of layman.

Let's be honest. Everyone else writing about the creation/evolution standoff is an expert. They know it and you know it. I, on the other hand, know almost nothing. My plan is to start at the bottom and work my way up to respectability. If the Genesis versus Darwin debate is a tug 'o war between two highly qualified factions, with the giants of discovery and invention on the left, and men and women of the cloth on the right—I am fully qualified to be the rope.

While I have always been able to defend my belief in the God of the Bible, I have sometimes struggled to make my faith fit with the God of Nature. I think this is true for many people who call themselves Christians. Trying to share my reasons for God, while pointing into the Petri dish of Creationism (or Intelligent Design as it has been rebranded) has made the task even tougher.

My lifelong fascination with Genesis and the ongoing debate about how we humans made it to this point in the universe continues to be simply that—a fascination. (Some guys collect riding mowers or rental property in Phoenix. I lay awake wondering if Cain's wife was more than just the girl next door with a knack for making great falafels.)

As my passion for this subject of origins has grown, I have unexpectedly lost myself sitting amidst stacks of used bookstore treasures, tattered notebooks and scribbled musings about life, logic and the nature of things. And I have also found contentment processing my faith and discovering how it sparks against the metal of a complex world of equations and atoms. My resulting take on the creation/evolution skirmish is the result of both theological meanderings and some ill-advised late night snacking. But the resulting "Aha!" moments have paved the way for inspired and intense chatter with both friends and skeptics.

While my home office exhibits considerable evidence of chaos and my sock drawer only hints at order and design, I've always been convinced that the universe makes sense because it's supposed to. The heavens do, without any doubt in my mind, declare loudly and boldly the glory of God. And that's a good thing because I can be hard of hearing. For too much of my adult life I've suffered from self-inflicted ignorance—an unwillingness to ask the big questions, the scary questions.

My concern is for more than my own faith journey. I have two daughters who are currently neck deep in the educational system. I want my kids—I want everyone's kids to understand that the science lab is to be feared but not ignored. People don't kill people. Bunsen burners kill people.

"Letters from the Slippery Slope" is my story. I'm on an adventure to rediscover my faith without accidentally tossing any of the good stuff. Some people tell me that this may be the dumbest thing I have ever attempted and I'd like to prove them wrong. This may not even rank in the top ten. I have decided to record my findings and observations while I attempt to sort out the contentious issues that make the faith versus reason argument so compelling to many of us. I'm going to talk to experts and idiots alike. Eventually, I hope to be able to tell the difference between the two.

For those readers who reside with the skeptics on the evolutionary side of the fence in this debate—you will be disappointed to learn that I have not abandoned my faith. Some of you, comfortably ensconced in the same evangelical camp that I grew up in, may come to the conclusion that I have either lost my salvation or perhaps never had it.

My attempt to embrace both the book of nature, as interpreted by science, and the books of revelation, what we call the Bible, is just that. An attempt. I'm still figuring it out. If it's true that faith without works is dead, it may also be true that faith that doesn't work, doesn't mesh with the real world, will soon be left for dead. I sincerely hope that this record of my struggles, frustrations and discoveries will revive the faith of some and breathe life into others who have been enduring an existence of grey matter alone.

Perhaps you've picked up this book because you're attracted by the voracity of the debate but not so sure you're up for a strenuous journey onto the slippery slope. Relax. Come along for the ride. There's no peddling required; it's pretty much down hill the whole way. If you've read this far already it's too late to get a refund so your only options are to keep going or re-gift this thing to the pimply guy who changes your oil. Might as well keep reading. What's the worst thing that could happen?

1

STORM WARNING

I t was the eleventh month in the year 2007, as we tell time from our vantage point in the universe. Albert Einstein's theory of relativity with its mind-bending tales of black holes and photons was about ninety years old. *On The Origin of Species by Means of Natural Selection* by Charles Darwin, first published in 1859, was 146 years old. It had been 361 years since Galileo had been placed under house arrest for suggesting that the earth might not be the exact centre of the universe.

However, all I was thinking about at this moment was that I was cold and drenched, but safe from the pounding rain in a cozy pub on the west side of Vancouver, B.C. What I didn't know was that right here, tonight, my highly ordered world was about to go sideways.

I peeled off my navy blue shell, shook the rain onto the battered hardwood and hung it from a dented brass hook near my table. I gazed across a restaurant crammed with the tousled heads of university students and assorted locals to a flat panel screen mounted over the bar. Distorted figures danced, shape-shifting like bodies in a midway fun-house mirror to the strains of "Denial Twist" by the White Stripes. Cool tune. Happy conversations reverberated off the tired oak paneling, a sure sign that tonight's patrons were enjoying their respite from another wet winter on the west coast.

We don't get hurricanes in Vancouver. At least nothing like the category fours and fives that CNN broadcasts into my living room. Vancouver likely gets all the water of a Katrina, but none of the drama. I'd grown up in this city and was fully adapted or had become immune to the unrelenting winter rains.

I settled into a corner booth along with a group of nine other musicians. We had just finished playing a set of worship music at a cozy Baptist church near the University of British Columbia. Soulful voices, fiddle and guitar, bass and Gibson electric, Hammond organ and accordion were still reverberating in my head. The drums, now only an echo, lent a rhythmic cadence to my reading of the pub menu. The music wouldn't fade away until I was asleep later that night.

The sound of the rain, however, was unlikely to stop. The rain would always be there. Before I'd even dried off from the dash between church and pub (a journey I had made rarely over the course of my life) I was hovering over a mushroom burger and a pile of sizzling onion rings. I offered one to the guy sitting across from me.

I had only known Dan, the leader of our worship band, for a few weeks and didn't have a full read on him yet. The first night I showed up at his church, I overheard a couple laughing and refer to him as Jesus. They were referring to his shoulder-length hair, fair skin, two day old beard and penetrating blue eyes that would put him at the front of any casting call line-up should Andrew Lloyd Webber drag *Jesus Christ Superstar* out of the mothballs. Yes, Dan was a very convincing Caucasian Jesus once you got past the paint-smeared navy gym shorts, red striped woolen work socks, and cross-trainers. He always changed into jeans and a plaid shirt before we started playing, but I suspected he lived out the balance of his week in those ragged shorts.

Dan and I started jawing like musicians tend to do after every gig. (I'm not sure if gig carries the weight of conservative orthodoxy, but usual church words like music ministry are too full of hymnbook dust and polyester.) We discussed which songs worked the best and why the lyrics on the screen never match those on lead sheets. We wondered what causes a drumstick to take flight in the direction of the baptismal tank. And we talked hockey.

As other conversations and punch lines buzzed around us, I asked Dan what he did for work. He replied that he was a geologist, a soils engineer to be precise.

"And you can make a living at that?" I asked.

"You would be amazed at how much money people throw at me to go up north for a few weeks and dig around," he answered before proceeding with a summary on the current state of geo-technical life—soil engineering, slope sustainability, environmental assessment—and what it was like to commute to work in a float plane, camp for real money and lie awake at night listening for bears.

While I was fascinated with his impromptu expose on the life of a geologist in the Canadian North, I found myself distracted by a short list of questions forming in my mind. Did he agree with the biblical narrative that stated the universe was created in seven literal twenty-four hour days? (Well, six days, with one left over for church and football). I also wanted to ask if in his geologically attuned opinion, dinosaurs ever roamed the earth at the same time as humans. Some of the young earth creationists I'd read supported this notion. I was pretty sure Dan wouldn't qualify himself as a young earth creationist which would leave him on the intelligent design side of the chronological fence. (Intelligent design advocates were also creationists, but allowed for a whole lot more time to pass in the early verses of Genesis.)

Dan paused for a moment when his dinner arrived and I took the opportunity to pounce.

"So... are you a... a young earth creationist?" I asked. I took a bite of my burger and waited for his reply. And I waited.

Dan said nothing as he looked over my shoulder, beyond our booth to the door, where more soaked patrons were scurrying out of the elements. "How many days has it been raining?" he asked.

"Why?" I replied, "You thinking of building an ark?"

Dan smiled, and reached for the ketchup. He didn't offer an answer. As I considered myself proficient in matters concerning both creation and Genesis and was more than mildly curious, I thought I'd push the issue.

"You're a creationist right? An 'intelligent design' guy?" After a long silence... and a sigh, he looked at me with his Jesus eyes.

"I'm a geologist," he said. "I've been studying rocks and soils my whole life, and there is absolutely no chance the earth is only ten thousand or ten million or one hundred million years old."

Dan kept talking, but I only remember hearing the words "not very dogmatic" before something like panic overpowered my frontal lobe and shut down my ear canals. I felt a blanket, invisible and suffocating as sandwich wrap, snaking around my skull like a bandage being applied to a gaping head wound. First my ears, and then my lower jaw lost function. My throat tightened. "Keep calm," I told myself. "Chew. Smile. Don't gag." Had I heard this guy correctly? Did he really intend for those words to come out of his mouth?

I would have asked Dan to clarify his position, but my tongue had given up speech and was searching for my uvula. Was he aware of the damage he had inflicted with his flippant answer? Christians can be so careless with their words.

I quickly diagnosed the swirling sensation that had me paralyzed in my seat as either a panic attack or a stroke. Suddenly I was aware of every conversation in the entire restaurant, all thirty-eight of them, amidst the thrashing of cutlery and the muted growl of food being crushed by jawbones. Bodies around me now moved in slow motion. I stared blankly as salt and pepper shakers were passed hand by hand in response to a chicken pot pie crisis at the other end of our table. Although I was unable to process the pandemonium playing out before me, I did manage to replay the last words I could remember Dan speaking— "I'm a geologist... I've studied rocks and soil my whole life... there is absolutely no chance the earth is only ten thousand or even ten million or one hundred million years old."

I'd like to believe that Dan and the other musicians at our table didn't notice any change in my demeanor. After all, I was a preacher's kid and we are notoriously brilliant at faking it. I took another bite and kept chewing, but I couldn't taste my food. Dan spoke again, only this time in hushed tones.

"I don't like to talk about it," he said cautiously between bites. "Causes a lot of tension and doesn't solve anything. I would rather not go there."

He looked away and then turned his attention to his plate, unaware that even in this state of partial paralysis and with my dominant hand gripping my burger I still had full range of motion in my right shoulder, and a fully loaded fork at the ready. But stabbing Dan wouldn't solve anything, I told myself. Besides, it would be bad for band morale. I didn't know what to do next. Either my entire Christian worldview had just been challenged by this soil-loving hippie or I had suddenly developed an allergic reaction to mayonnaise. Whatever it was, I was reeling. I struggled to find the words… something charitable to say. No words came.

I have been told by witnesses to that conversation that the discussion retreated to safer ground for the balance of the evening, but I don't remember. I ate in silence, sifting through the wreckage of a conversation that held so much promise before my new friend took dead aim at Genesis, at the foundations of everything I knew about my faith, and I had been forced to hit the eject button. My creationist sensibilities had been violated, and I couldn't wait for my drive back across town to the suburbs, where faith and sanity reigned.

Depression, an emotion foreign to me, began gnawing at my gut as I reached for my jacket, paid my bill and ventured back out into the rain. An unwelcome chill draped over me like a haunting November fog as I drove away under the mocking glare of streetlights shining from high above the windshield of my tiny Toyota. The pounding of windshield wipers failed to keep pace with the storm of emotions inside me. I scowled at the speedometer, ground my teeth and eased up on the gas.

I drove for almost an hour.

Disconnected.

Robotic.

Down Twelfth Avenue, past City Hall, through the streets of East Vancouver, onto the freeway, skirting two municipalities, over the Fraser River and finally home. While the cold Vancouver rain would continue for another forty days, a deadening numbness, a spiritual hypothermia, something I'd never experienced before, was only beginning to settle in.

§

I think a lot. On the good days it's a pleasant way to be, but on the not so good days it's not so good. Sort of like a can of spray paint that's been shaken. Things might look stable on the outside, but the molecules inside are taking a beating, and there isn't enough space to keep all the angry particles isolated from each other. And as long as there is someone nearby to keep shaking the can, the molecules will remain agitated.

I wasn't even sure how to begin processing the conversation from that night in the pub. For starters, I didn't know if I could keep dragging my keyboard gear all the way across town to play in a worship band where this guy—an apostate Jesus look-a-like, a pied piper in navy gym shorts—was leading an unsuspecting parade of college students and impressionable teens like lambs to the theological slaughter. Had I unknowingly become an instrument of darkness? Fortunately, they didn't record the band that night, so we'll never know for sure.

How is it possible for a person to call himself a Christian, to accept Jesus' claim as the Son of God as recorded in the New Testament writings, and at the same time hold to an 'expert' opinion that God didn't create the world as is stated so clearly in Genesis chapter one of the Old Testament? I knew that Adam and Eve, created by God and placed in the Garden of Eden, were the first in a long line of historical figures. I knew that according to biblical chronology, they lived less than ten thousand years ago. If the creation story, pulled directly from the early chapters of Genesis (and the human chronology that follows later in Genesis) doesn't count for anything—isn't trustworthy—what makes the rest of the Bible worth contemplating at all?

In the days and weeks that followed that conversation with my musician friend Dan, questions like these were never far from the surface. My only recourse was to attempt to wring some logic out of Dan's polite ambush. I didn't know it yet, but my allegiance to a faith perspective—an entrenched theological position that pitted the authority of Holy Scripture against the accuracy of scientific discovery—was about to be tested beyond belief.

2

YOU DON'T KNOW JACK

One day Jack arrived. He was the new IT guy at our company. Jack isn't a Christian. Many of his favorite words have four letters in them, although he does have some dandies that run over by a couple of vowels and a consonant cluster. Jack speaks with a thick Polish accent, a result of spending the first seventeen years of his life in Poland, his final months running from gunfire in the streets of Warsaw. (Clarification: the thick Polish accent is in no way a result of the gun episode.) After high school, and a couple of years bumming around Greece picking fruit, Jack made his way to Canada and settled in Vancouver.

Jack told me that as a young adult in a communist eastern European nation, he had free access to a carton of cigarettes and two bottles of Vodka every month. Sort of a "Hey, you're still here—have a drink!" rewards program for the loyal citizenry. (In Canada, we tax our cigarettes to pay for our health care system, which is ironic since few people who take up smoking live long enough to see all that tax revenue at work.)

To suggest that Jack's upbringing was different from mine is an understatement. I grew up in a house where we kids got sent to our room for coming home from the store with candy cigarettes. But if we were good we could get out of bed at midnight and join Mom and Dad at the kitchen table for cinnamon toast and hot chocolate. "Hey, you're still here—have a drink!"

From the first day he arrived, Jack made quite an impression on company culture. He has strong opinions on politics, technology, gun control, sex and religion. At our polite little company we only talked about four of those five topics, which left Jack with plenty of dead air to occupy when it was his turn to carry the conversation. I was skeptical this working arrangement was going to last. We were all so... well, conservative, and based on first impressions, our new IT guy was anything but. After only a few days, Jack discovered that I was a f***ing Christian (his words more or less). And he was quick to inform anyone within earshot that he was a f***ing atheist. However, contrary to all my predictions, Jack survived probation, likely because he was very good at his job and despite the fact that he had this annoying habit of telling us exactly what he was thinking—whether we wanted to hear it or not. Considering I spend a lot of time around people of faith, I found his ruthless honesty bizarre and refreshing.

One morning, I found myself wrapped up in a conversation with Jack and I wasn't even part of it. I was an innocent bystander when he began a typical IT support phone call with a co-worker based in the U.S. As it was several weeks before the presidential election, Jack thought it would be fun to take an impromptu poll of the electorate.

"Who are you going to vote for?" I heard him ask in his thick eastern European accent. I could tell by his tone that he was speaking with a woman.

"Don't go there," came a whisper from an adjoining cubicle. Then a snicker. It was Steve, a co-worker. I pulled my hands away from my computer keyboard and leaned backwards, straining to hear what would come next. Did I mention that Jack has the remarkable habit of telling you what he thinks, whether or not you want to hear it?

"Oh, I see," said Jack to the voice on the other end of the line. "You're going to vote for the Christian candidate. And who is that?"

"You're not going to like the answer." More commentary from Steve. I sat silently, listening in disbelief to a conversation headed the wrong way in a hurry.

"Why does it matter if he's a Christian or not... as long as he can get the job done?" Steve tried to intervene. His words suggested a call for caution but his tone signaled resignation. Jack attempted to continue his interrogation of the mystery caller, but the tables suddenly turned.

"Am I a Christian? Nope. I grew up Catholic in Poland, but now I'm... I'm nothing! But there are two very indoctrinated Christian guys sitting next to me in this office RIGHT NOW and I'm pretty sure they don't think that either presidential candidate is the antichrist." Jack's voice was dripping with glee.

"Here's what I believe," said Jack. "I believe that as long as I'm a good person and I don't shoot nobody..." (That Warsaw thing again.)

"What? Do I believe in evolution? Of course! What's not to believe?"

I was about to burst like a cheap paper funnel. I felt like I was sitting on the bench during the most important football game of the year and I was stuck on the wrong sideline! I found myself hoping, even praying that my atheist friend wouldn't be handed yet another reason to laugh at my faith and NOT believe. I considered racing next door, grabbing the receiver out of his hand and yelling into the phone at whoever it was on the other end "Are you kidding? ARE YOU KIDDING ME? Since when did NOT believing in evolution find its way into the Apostle's Creed?" but I managed to stay in my chair.

I sure didn't believe in evolution, but I would never consider launching into the deep end of a faith conversation with a rant against Darwin's idea as the lynchpin to my apologetic.

Over the next two and a half minutes, the voice on the other of the line explained to Jack what you had to believe if you wanted to be a Christian. I could only gather by Jack's quick responses that young earth creationism had taken its proper place on the catwalk of fashionable faith positions somewhere between original sin and the Trinity. A ten thousand year old earth was in. Troodons and triceratops were out. Whatever was coming over the phone line was not going to impress Jack. I listened harder as my brow tensed and then cramped up.

"Well, tell me this," said Jack with added inflection and volume, guessing that by now I had abandoned my desk chair for a better listening post. My good ear was plastered to our adjoining office wall like bark on a California redwood.

"Do you believe in dinosaurs?" he said. "Oh… So you don't believe in dinosaurs. Okay, now we're getting somewhere!"

I exhaled slowly, peeled my sorry self off of the flat grey drywall and slumped down in my office chair.

Moments later, after a polite end to the service call, Jack appeared at my office door. He carried a menacing grin that danced under a pair of thick black Euro frames straining to hold the bewilderment in his eyes. I looked away, feigning nonchalance, but it was no use pretending I hadn't heard. I steadied myself for the hellish barrage of insults I knew was coming, flaming darts from the tongue of an accuser decked out in metro-sexual plaid pants and stylish Italian shoes.

"Calvin…" Jack's presence filled the doorway. He would let the silence do all the work. "You didn't tell me you don't believe in dinosaurs," he said gently, as though he were scolding a child who'd been caught with Lego up his nose. He stepped forward, invading what little space remained between us.

"But I do believe in dinosaurs," I replied boldly.

"Bull**it!" he shot back. "This lady on the phone says that she's a Christian and doesn't believe in dinosaurs. Ah…" Jack buried his head in his hands as he flopped into an empty chair across from my desk. His lips were moving—he was mumbling under his breath and in less than two seconds he had successfully sequenced the four letters that he would use to get my attention.

"We don't all believe the identical things," I responded weakly. "I think the reformers called it wiggle room."

"These Fundamentalist Christians are crazy," he said, waving his hands over his head like he was spinning plates.

"Crazy might be a little strong," I said.

"You think so?" said Jack.

"You have to understand church culture…" I started to say before he cut me off.

"Crazy is exactly the word! I say we collect up the whole lot and shoot them before they infect us with their stupid genes. If we could have about twenty years without any religion, now that would fix everything!"

"Didn't Stalin try that?" I asked. Poles have a highly developed little brother complex about the Russians, very similar to the Canadian-American dynamic. I sat back in silent approval at my insightful jab.

"How did that work out, Jack?"

"Okay—you got me on that." He huffed and cursed under his breath as he scrambled out of the chair and stormed back to his desk.

§

What I learned in the following months of working with Jack was that he was a skeptic, a liberals' liberal, and a free thinker. I also discovered (unbeknownst to Jack) that while my initial responses to his questions about God and Christianity were coherent, my stock supply of answers to questions about Genesis and the flood, and Adam and Eve, were not going to cut it. Not with this guy. It's not that I was afraid of getting into an argument with him, or worried that he'd crawl under my desk and sabotage my Mac. Ok, so maybe I was a little worried that he'd crawl under my desk and sabotage my Mac. I just didn't want to spoil any of our productive God talks by spewing some ill-timed origins comments out into the ether. I was a creationist after all; I knew that God had created the heavens and the earth just like it says in Genesis. But I wanted to make sure I broke the news to Jack slowly. So I held my tongue. Didn't give him anything. I knew Jack well enough by this time to know unless I could come up with some deeper, more articulate answers about how the Bible related to science, our fiery water cooler conversations about faith were going to be severely dampened.

I so wanted there to be a way to bridge the chasm between his understandings of the real world and mine. I needed, for the sake of my own faith, and for reasons I couldn't even articulate yet, to make a conscious effort to put my views about origins "on hold" for a few weeks. What would happen if I crawled behind enemy lines to investigate the creation/evolution argument from the other side? I owed it to Jack to give him the best answer I could come up with. I owed it to myself. I was almost certain that the line in the sand dividing faith from science would survive my messing about. To take such a step might be dangerous. I had no idea what lies or half-truths would be waiting to trip me up. I wasn't sure if this curious endeavor would strengthen my journey of faith or derail it with a fool's rationale. But I had a sense that by the time I was through, I was going to discover some new things about why I believed what I believed.

Since that rainy night in the pub with my musician friend Dan, I had been slowly reclaiming my sense of equilibrium. The vertigo was history now, and I was looking forward to the prospect of re-learning or unlearning some things about the way I might be able to integrate my faith with the scientific corner of my brain. I wasn't exactly sure where to start, or what rabbit trails or tangents I'd discover along the way, but I knew one thing for sure—over the entire course of the human story, God has proved extremely competent at steering his children back onto the right path whenever we've wandered too close to the edge.

I didn't know whether I was trying to convert Jack's intellect or simply learn some respect for his skepticism, but I decided that for Jack, for the sake of the gospel, I would become an honorary "temporary" evolutionist. At least I could give it a try.

3

THE SLIPPERY SLOPE

"It's a slippery slope," said a former Bible college instructor when I suggested attending a free lecture on origins at a theology school across town.

"That is a very slippery slope indeed—you'd better watch yourself!" said a co-worker with evangelical fire in his eyes. All I had done was bring up the notion of Noah's flood being less universal than, say, Coke.

This infamous slippery slope is a difficult place, it turns out, to pin down on a map, and its rumored existence brings up a host of intriguing questions. For instance, how do you know if you've discovered a slippery slope? Is it steep like the roof on a prairie barn or gentle like silk sheets on a gimpy futon? Why is it slippery? How far can one slide on a slippery slope? How far down am I already? What kind of gear would I need before I could venture out safely onto this hazardous hypotenuse? Hiking boots? Ropes and carabineers? Flares? Snacks? What about snacks? Wouldn't want to get stranded in the bottom of a theological canyon without graham wafers and trail mix.

And is it true that nothing good, only pain and incontrovertible grief, awaits the fool who dares take a leisurely stroll on a slippery slope in the first place? Do those high school vector equations which prove that putting one's weight on an inclined plane without having adequate surface tension to maintain one's position on said plane still apply if you are exercising your faith and praying really hard?

According to the legal experts, a slippery slope can exist in one of two possible states, either causally or semantically. A "causal" slippery slope is the logical end result, we'll call it point Z, of an action we'll call point A. If we start by considering point A as a topic of conversation, eventually we will accept point A as valid, then point B, C D etc. until we find ourselves in a terrible place, point Z (zeta in Spanish). A wasteland of regret in any language, a morass of abject hopelessness.

An example is in order.

If I announced that launching dogs into space is a bad idea and you agreed, we would call that point Z. However, what if you then proposed that instead of launching them into space, we simply allowed pet owners to bring their labradoodles to Cape Canaveral and pay us twenty bucks for an 8"x10" glossy of Fido resting comfortably in the cockpit of the Space Shuttle? Well, I could either agree with your brilliant idea, or oppose it based on the fact that while a twenty-dollar photo seems harmless enough (point A), it's only a matter of time before a very wealthy dog owner shows up with a check for $100,000 and demands that we launch Buzz, his prize-winning pug, into orbit (point Z). I would play the slippery slope card and accuse you of opening the doggie door to unethical canine space travel.

The other type of slippery slope is of the semantic variety and can be explained thus: Since there is no definitive line, either legally or morally, to separate tall from short, for an intelligent person in the twenty-first century to take the position of being either tall or short is both arbitrary and irresponsible. Tallness or shortness as a state of being is not worthy of serious discussion since we can't actually know from our vantage point in the universe whether we are tall or short.

However, there are some among us (amusement park sign painters) who profess to have inside knowledge and try to dictate to us, the paying customers, exactly where tall becomes short. I wouldn't be surprised if they've been coached by amusement park lawyers on this—and we know how much lawyers love slippery slopes. The real difficulty comes in determining exactly where along the continuum short ceases being short and morphs into tall. Was Goliath tall? The correct answer is probably. But would you ever know by lining him up against the gym wall with his other Philistine schoolmates? Was David short? Well, he was able to pick out five smooth stones for his sling-shot, which constitutes undeniable proof of the nearness of his eyeballs to the stream bed, but it is also possible that he was crouching down.

Another Old Testament character, Esau, was extremely hairy. His brother Jacob was not. The question that has eluded Bible scholars to centuries is: exactly how many hairs must one be lacking in any given square inch of epidermis to be considered bald? The Bible doesn't tell us. We are left to work this out on our own, and waxing is not an option.

Tall.

Short.

Hairy.

Bald.

These are all examples of semantic slippery slopes. Which leaves us exactly where?

For my journey into the evolution-creation debate, the causal slippery slope, the first definition applies. At least it applies until we get to Darwin's bit about the monkeys—where the issues of hairy and short become more than mildly relevant.

The accusation of causal slippery-sloped-ness often surfaces during a heated debate surrounding interpretation of Scripture. I am familiar with the argument from the perspective of a young earth creationist and should have been prepared for the anger hurled my way once I ventured over to the dark side. Recent conversations have included comments from fellow believers that border on insulting, accusatory and downright nasty. And that's just when I'm talking to my mom!

Family squabbling aside, the accusations take a familiar shape: Your first mistake, says the creationist, is to let science dictate the conversation by allowing them to have their billions of years for the age of the universe.

Then they'll ask us to cave on the hundreds of millions of years of life on this planet so they can push their evolution. Give 'em an era and they'll take an eon! Before we know what has hit us (THEY say it was an asteroid 65 millions years ago) Adam and Eve have been written out of the story. And Noah's flood. But the nonsense doesn't just stop there. The slippery slope never sleeps. Before we can summon any witnesses to the stand, the miracles of Jesus get thrown out on a technicality, and then the final nail in the coffin: the resurrection story itself gets buried. All because we went soft on creation as it is laid out plainly in Genesis.

For believers on the creationist side of the debate the stakes are life and death: We have to make our stand at Genesis or we lose everything. Even a polite attempt at reconciliation between biblical faith and science is not worth the risk. For most of my Christian life, I have maintained that a literal understanding of the Bible is the surest way to avoid the slippery slope. And until now that advice has served me well.

Truth is, I've been afraid of the other story. You know, the one about oozing pond scum that springs into action, deciding after hundreds of millions of years that it doesn't like the water anymore, so it grows legs and moves into a cute bungalow in the valley before realizing that the water wasn't so bad, at which point it posts all its earthly belongings on Craigslist and rolls back into the ditch to continue a meaningless existence of mutating and shaping its own earlobes for millennia ad infinitum until WOW here we are lounging around on Facebook eating flash-frozen shrimp from a big box retailer—all the while meditating on why we suck at being kinder, gentler *Homo sapiens*.

Yeah! That story.

I had never considered that there might be a coherent "other" position to take on the matter until that disturbing confrontation with my geologist friend Dan a few months back. A recent series of unsettling chats with non-believing friends and an atheist co-worker had left me shaken. Those conversations weren't going to get any easier by themselves. Now, with this persistent, gnawing sensation in my gut, in my soul, I didn't see any other way to the other side of this canyon than by the most direct route.

Somewhere down there in the muck, buried beneath the sediment of tradition and translation and dogma, was an answer—a missing link of sorts—that might explain this theological ache that now followed me every waking moment.

I felt a little bit like Edmund Pevensie in the Narnia Chronicles of C.S. Lewis. There was only one way to know with certainty that Lucy was telling the truth. I would have to crawl up into the attic, step bravely into the imposing wardrobe of science, and feel my way through the furs hanging in the darkness to see if Narnia really existed. If upon closer inspection of the facts I became convinced that the secular view of our human origins wasn't sound science, then I wouldn't have lost anything. At worst, I would have gained a heightened understanding of the concepts being paraded around by the skeptics and atheists. And I'd likely have some idea of how to refute them.

However, if Narnia did exist, there wasn't anything that I'd be able to do to make it vanish. If Narnia was real... well, it wouldn't be a surprise to God. If the imaginary world of the evolutionists was real, and the Bible was also true... WAIT! They can't both be true.

Can they?

4

BLAME IT ON FLANNELGRAPH

I n the middle ages, Church leaders found themselves unable to accept Galileo's notion of a heliocentric universe. Psalm 104:5 states clearly, "He set the earth on its foundations; it can never be moved." To suggest that the earth rotated around the sun was crackpot science at best, heresy at worst. Eight years of house arrest suggests that Galileo was considered more than a crackpot.

But I'm not about to lay blame with the ancient scribes who were forced to write painstakingly with kosher quill and freshly mixed ink every word of the Hebrew Scriptures (also known as the Torah or Old Testament to Christians) onto handmade parchment, only to have it shred like Savoy cabbage in the photocopier. No, if I'm going to point an accusing finger at any player in this ages old science/faith fiasco, I need to look no further than my own Sunday school upbringing.

I call FLANNELGRAPH to take the stand.

For those who've forgotten about flannelgraph or didn't attend Sunday school in the seventies or eighties, let me bring you up to speed. Flannelgraph is exactly like Velcro except it contains absolutely none of the industrial-strength properties that make Velcro so useful. But it is colorful and fluffy, just like those pajamas you wore as a kid. The best part was that if you ran out of store-bought Bible characters and animals, you could cut up your sister's nightgown into almost any shape, including clouds, trees, rocks, sheep, tigers, serpents, Adam and Eve and, of course, fig leaves. These flannel pieces would cling to a big flannel-friendly board mounted to the wall of your Sunday school classroom. Back in the day, before video projectors and iPods had taken over, flannelgraph was it.

In those days all Sunday school teachers were sent away to a secret location where they were trained in the ancient flannelgraphic arts. These storytelling, textile hurling ninjas were capable of reciting a Bible story while looking you right in the eye, while their right hand dragged multi-colored flannel icons out of an old shoe box and their left hand slapped said icons onto the flannel board with dizzying speed and questionable accuracy. It was a 50/50 cotton-blend blur of inspired proportions.

You and your classmates would sit, glued to your tiny plastic chairs (yes, glued—one of many flannelgraph artist tricks) while your teacher created, as if by magic, a four foot wide reconstruction of the actual garden of Eden. And you would remember every detail of this masterpiece until the car ride home when your mom asked what you learned in Sunday School today and you would say, "We ate marshmallows and Mike can blow snot bubbles." But you did remember—every detail.

How could the impressionable seven-year-old mind ever forget the images of a lush, fertile garden in the heart of a Mesopotamian valley, adorned in lime-green pinstriped junipers and blue tartan palm trees that towered nearly twice as tall as Adam and Eve in their matching zebra skin cave gear? And there was an apple, not just any apple, but the fourteen pound apple that Eve was about to eat, perched menacingly in the branches of a mid-western American red oak tree, about to fall on a small herd of checkerboard yaks that had surrounded a lonesome baby giraffe only a few paces across the garden from the scary angel with the flaming sword. Poor baby giraffe with the orange paisley coat. And it's no wonder the serpent is smiling. The serpent is smiling because a blue, striped crocodile is lying upside down in a chronologically whacked out polka dot manger left over from last week's lesson. And at the teacher's feet, Tony Sabato, the Italian kid who was sitting right beside you until a moment ago when he wiggled out of his pants which are still glued to his chair, is trying to rip the matching zebra skin cave gear off Adam and Eve because he can't stop himself.

Truth is, you never forget those images. You just forget that you remembered them. Years later, when you're twelve, you still have dozens of these files—images of fuzzy pajama animals lying dormant in that part of your brain where the flannel neurons hibernate. But you don't know they're in there. And it's day nineteen of the biology module in seventh grade science class, and you're trying to be cool, and you're lucky enough to have scored a seat in the lab next to Jennifer Martin, and your biology teacher points to you and asks a question.

It's a simple question really—something about hollow bones and a dinosaur femur. One that you should be able to answer without a moment's hesitation because you've just spent the last week and a half cooped up in a smelly classroom with twenty-three other kids dissecting chickens. You are a budding expert in avian anatomy. You know that a chicken skeleton has 307 bones and can be reassembled with 4.75 bottles of Elmer's Glue-All. You know precisely where the optic nerve of an American Leghorn Rooster attaches to the brain. You also know from experience that this optic nerve will follow the same trajectory as any other elastic compound stretched to the breaking point and launched against the classroom window. You know what a spleen smells like. And you know you'll never go near KFC again as long as you live.

And so you attempt to answer the question when suddenly, out of the recesses of your twelve-year-old testosterone-broiled mind, you spot a parade of pink and green plaid flannel alpacas, dancing two by two over the blackboard at the front of the classroom. You reach your hands out and try to swat them away. You pray that no one else sees them. You pray that God will pull from the recesses of your short-term memory just one tiny chicken fact. Something, anything, that might be true about this chicken that you've spent nine days getting to know way more than any chicken needs to be known. And your mouth goes dry. And you know God is real, and he's in your heart and your science teacher is wrong and there is absolutely no way that this chicken is related to a Tyrannosaurus rex.

The worst part is that you know you'll endure some serious mocking if you say anything out loud. So you never admit to anyone that you don't believe any of this science stuff, except for the physics equations you studied before Easter break. These teachers don't even go to church, so they can't be right. They just can't be. Being right about science stuff is for Christians.

5

A WALK IN THE PARK – PART 1

s the earth opened up and swallowed my car whole, I stood on the brake pedal to keep my reckless descent into the canyon from turning nasty. In an instant I had been jettisoned from the vibrant Alberta prairie into a seemingly dead and dusty wilderness—a relic from another era.

Dinosaur Provincial Park, located two hours east of the Calgary Airport, was my intended destination. According to the map spread out on the passenger seat, this park was supposed to be green. If this place had been anything like the provincial parks on the coast I would have seen it coming, announced by a stand of towering evergreens or a gnarled cedar stump the size of my garage. That's how you identify a park where I come from. I was not prepared for such a rude welcome to so famous a landmark.

Only moments earlier I had been cruising at eighty miles an hour, stereo dialed up to stun, as my weekend rental hurtled towards the horizon. Fortunately, the car clung to the pavement as it fell away beneath my tires, snaking onto the south bank of the Red Deer River Valley. If not for the persistent tug of gravity, a picnic table piled high with unsuspecting campers would have witnessed the surprise launch of a late model Malibu from the surface of Township Road 210A into the north bank of this river basin. While I did manage to keep the car under control, I ended up in the gravel more than once as my eyes darted in all directions, absorbing the sudden shift in terrain.

As quickly as I had vanished from the prairie skyline and dropped into the chilly September shadows of the Alberta badlands, my sense of adventure turned cold. Almost embedding a car in the wall of a canyon will do that to a person. What was I hoping to accomplish out here anyway? For the next eight hours I would be sequestered in a lonesome canyon under the hot sun, with nothing but a tool pack, industrial strength bug spray, and a vanload of dusty tourists. Paleontology hacks, all of us. I had paid good money to become a willing participant in the continuing search for pieces to an ancient puzzle. I was going on a dinosaur dig.

Did I really believe that chasing a paleontologist like a lost puppy, backpack full of water bottles and cranium wrapped in a Tilley hat to ward off a terminal case of Alberta redneck, was going to get me anything more than chapped lips? Was this scheme, hatched only ten days ago, when my wife reminded me winter comes early on the east side of the Rockies, going to silence the questions that had dogged me for the last two and a half years? Questions of science and history, geologic columns and molecular clocks, faith and biblical interpretation, Darwin, Dawkins, and Genesis, had kept me awake and searching into the early hours for more nights than I could remember.

My car settled onto the canyon floor shortly after the speedometer had dropped into double digits. Another question in need of an urgent response weighed on my mind. Did anybody in Alberta unlock the public restrooms before 8:00 am? I stepped into an empty parking lot and began to pace.

I surveyed the small coulee that surrounded an angular sandstone-colored building that housed the park's information centre. Waist-high grass spilling out of dusty outcroppings swayed against the early morning wind, tempting me to venture closer. But I knew better. I knew that this valley would be well stocked with rattlesnakes, cactus and other terrors waiting for any unsuspecting city boy that dared venture into the brush. I decided to wait until park staff arrived. I knew it would be an even longer wait before I found any answers to my deeper questions today, if they came at all.

The Badlands of Alberta, home to the Royal Tyrell Museum in Drumheller, located two hours northwest along the same river that meandered through this dinosaur preserve, was home to one of the largest dinosaur collections in the world. I would be there tomorrow. This whirlwind adventure had become a priority as a detailed investigation of my creationist roots began to conflict with my curiosity to reconcile mainstream science with my faith. I was finally here. "This better be good," I muttered to no one in particular. I continued my tortured pacing in that lonely parking lot, all the while second-guessing how much fun one could have scrambling around ancient fossil bone-beds with a hobbling, grizzled old science hobbyist.

Suddenly, an olive green Jeep with a white Alberta logo on the fender raced into the parking lot from the backside of the visitors' centre and slid to a standstill on the dusty asphalt. A mud encrusted window dropped silently into the driver-side door.

"Calvin, is that you?" came a voice from behind the wheel. The voice was of a higher pitch than I had been expecting. I waved, grabbed my camera gear from a nearby bench and started for the jeep. A young woman, auburn braided pigtails dangling from a multi-colored knit skullcap, bounded out of the driver's seat.

"Hang tight for ten minutes," she said smiling. "I'll be right back" Before I had even said hello or asked about bathrooms, she had spun around, jumped right back into the jeep, and driven off in search of something scientific or edible. I hadn't been expecting this turn of events. How much fun could one really have scrambling around with a hobbling, grizzled old science hobbyist? Only Marie, the young French-Canadian undergrad leading today's little expedition, would be able to answer that question.

6

JUST A GUY THING?

My dad and I have been engaged in an ongoing theological discussion for almost two years now. It's more of a conversation than an argument, fueled by heavy doses of Tim Keller, N.T. Wright, and anyone else with a book title that gets our attention.

A few nights ago when my parents dropped in for a meal, Dad and I resumed our debate. After several volleys concerning the possible theological fallout of even attempting an evolutionary view of history, my dad froze mid-sentence and turned to my wife, who had called us all to attention. She was standing at the kitchen island holding a giant knife close to her throat, much like a microphone only way more unsettling. Arlene looked at my mom, and asked with all the frankness of a tabloid reporter, "So Gladys... What do you think about all this creation slash evolution talk? Does it matter to you how this all happened?"

My mom—who has spent the last forty-something years listening to her husband and eldest son debate everything from Bob Dylan's ill-fated foray into Christian Music to the obvious advantages of installing white shag carpet in a VW bug—replied, "It's a guy thing. Just let 'em talk it out.

Doesn't matter to me one way or the other!"

My mom sees the world in a way that discourages dissent. Her strawberry blonde hair, always impeccably coiffed in case the queen drops by for tea, is the only thing about her that isn't black and white. In fact, black and white stop and ask my mother for advice if they get lost and rumors start spreading about the appearance of grey.

"You mean just like climbing Everest?" asked Arlene. "So we should just let them climb the blasted thing and get it out of their system?"

Arlene wasn't tied emotionally or intellectually to any of my recent theological ramblings, and was awaiting the glorious day when my search for the answer to everything was over and I could get back to cleaning out the garage. When I had first told Arlene of my intention to take this journey she had been skeptical but supportive. She knows that if I made up my mind to reconstruct the entire human genome, all three billion base pairs, out of bleached Alphagetti and lay it out on an airport runway, nothing would deter me except a good nap. But my wife has also maintained since day one that none of this origins talk, which I've taken a shining to in recent months, plays a critical role in the faith conversation.

On the other hand, when my mom says "it doesn't matter to me one way or the other," what she really means is, "I don't care how long you toss these crazy ideas around, the Bible says God created the world in six days, and where's my knitting?"

"We live by faith, and not by sight," she's been known to say.

"Yes, but… having faith in something that isn't ultimately true doesn't get you any points. And we're not supposed to avoid using reason," I said. "All truth is God's truth."

"I don't think it's worth arguing about," she said.

"We're not arguing," I said. "We are simply debating whether it's too late in our tiny lives to tweak our worldview."

"But it just doesn't matter TO ME!" Arlene said emphatically as she continued waving the knife over her head, providing the trio of bell peppers on the cutting board a brief stay of execution.

"What do you mean it doesn't matter?" I asked, keeping my distance. "How can you have any confidence in the claims about Jesus being true if Genesis isn't settled? It may not matter to you personally, but this is the stuff that trips up a lot of skeptics."

"I don't think it's a deal-breaker," she said.

"Maybe not to you," I replied, jumping to my feet and then to my soapbox. "But to a lot of people who don't yet believe, they look at Christians like we're brain dead. For some people, the big questions concerning faith are the result of some traumatic event, such as a death in the family. One person loses a child and decides there can't be a God and the next person loses a child and they are driven towards the very idea of God as a sort of coping mechanism."

"But people don't come to faith in God because YOU convince them," said my mom.

"No, but SOME people (like my co-worker Jack) are hamstrung by logic, not just in spiritual things, but everything. They won't even give you the time of day unless that part of their brain that makes sense of life can see coherence between the biblical record and the real world. The scientific world. And a lot of Christians have done a pretty good job of making sure that's impossible."

"So you're saying that we should base our faith on the flavor of the month, whatever the scientists say it is?"

I sighed, more at my inability to articulate than the tone of the question.

"No… but a lot of Christians have set themselves up as judge and jury in a trial of scientific ideas when I'm not even sure we understand the science. Creationism has become a stumbling block to about five generations of deep thinkers, and I'm not sure we even see it."

"But what about MY FAITH?" said my mom, pausing to look up from her knitting.

"But does having faith mean you toss out your reasoning capacities?" I asked.

"It's just not that important TO ME," said my wife before attacking the peppers.

§

This is true. It isn't important to her. In recent months, we've developed the habit of reading to each other before shutting down for the night. The most common practice involves me reading out loud while she falls asleep. It's a great way to grow a relationship and enjoy quality time together without spending money. Apart from the cost of the book, it's a really cheap date.

However, this ritual does have its drawbacks. The first problem is that Arlene's literary tastes are nothing like mine. While I can become mesmerized reading a nine-page discourse on black holes and why we love them so much, my wife will be sleeping like a baby neutron star in under four minutes. So to balance off my soothing oral presentation of *A Brief History of Time* by Stephen Hawking, when it was her turn to read, she would take me on an Oprah approved, travel/cooking adventure in Tuscany. Who needs particle physics when you can learn to bake focaccia bread using only local ingredients and a wood burning oven that was commandeered by Marcus Aurelius to reheat lasagna before the Roman army broke camp and marched for Gaul? And then when it was my turn to read again, we would be spirited to far away places—planets so large that the differing flow of time results in eleven minutes passing there, while back on our planet, the locals have aged almost two years and... and she's out like a light again.

And so it went. On Tuesday night my wife would whisk me away to an exotic villa on the Mediterranean coastline in a savory search for the penultimate heather-basted duckling. And then on Wednesday night, I would open the pages of a more substantial offering and read spellbinding tales of dinosaur-dentistry gone wrong or learn how to reverse engineer a Tyrannosaurus rex from a chicken. And then on Thursday, it was her turn again, and I was left wondering why so many professional women intent on rediscovering their purpose and passion—ala Rick Warren—inevitably ended up in a flirty episode with a swarthy vintner named Gianni.

The second problem with our bizarre bedtime reading ritual was that I couldn't sleep after Arlene read to me. So without even trying I now know way more about springtime in Provence and the history of semolina flour than she knows about cosmic background radiation and molecular clocks. To be fair she actually stuck with me for long stretches during my first read through of Gerald Schroeder's *The Science of God*. But as the books kept piling up on my side of the bed, to the point where I couldn't reach the snooze alarm without dislocating my shoulder, I could tell she was losing focus. But catching more Zs.

Antony Flews' *There Is a God* made her eyes glaze over and *The Language of God* by Francis Collins was a great help when she contracted the flu as was indicated by the snoring. But *Flat Earth—The History of an Infamous Idea* by Christine Garwood just made her angry. Not at the author, but the fundamentalist characters involved with the Flat Earth Revival of the nineteenth and early twentieth centuries. Maybe there's hope for her yet.

§

One day I got to thinking. What if all this evolution/creation talk really is "just a guy thing"? When women say this, what they really mean is, "This may be the dumbest thing you've ever done." Mrs. Hillary had to eat those words after Sir Edmond arrived back from his little hike at the Everest property. And it couldn't have been easy for Isaac Newton's wife. He was so busy writing down the laws of interplanetary motion he couldn't even spare three minutes to write her a love poem. Thus, her name was never recorded and her identity is forever lost to history.

At least I had the decency to craft a song for my wife and have it sung at our wedding. Alas, it was never recorded and is forever lost to history.

Perhaps the male brain climbs, digs, collects, calculates and wrestles with issues of the natural world because we're hardwired by our creator to delve into the deepest mysteries of the universe and never settle for not knowing. Or it could be just a way of avoiding taking out the garbage. "Please Honeybun, surely it can wait until morning, I'm just tidying up the second law of thermodynamics!"

But it can't be just a guy thing, can it? Florence Nightingale was the founder of modern nursing technique and heroine of the Crimean war. She followed up her nursing accomplishments by inventing the pie chart. If a guy had done that, every PowerPoint slide would be loaded up with multi-colored "meat charts." And what about Florence Nightingale Graham? She changed her name when her cosmetics startup took off. We know her better as Elizabeth Arden. Perhaps the prime example of a woman's touch in scientific endeavor was Marie Curie. She dedicated her life, pressing on in spite of the untimely death of her husband, to the study of uranium and other radioactive compounds. She perfected the mobile X-ray machine to help medics and was touted as the most famous woman on the planet at the end of the World War One, and she didn't even have her own daytime talk show.

No one mentioned so far has blown anything up. What gives? It turns out that while Curie was finding ways of turning unstable elements into instruments for healing and life, an American physicist, J. Robert Oppenheimer, was leading a secretive group of atomic theorists in a race against the Nazi war machine to find ways of transforming stable elements into less than stable elements. The Manhattan Project, following the logic laid down in Albert Einstein's famous equation $E=MC^2$, managed to split one atom into many very tiny, very angry pieces. Definitely a GUY THING!

Around the same time, on the other side of the Atlantic, Werner Von Braun, a German rocketeer, was successful in his efforts to make pointy, shiny objects leave the ground, pull away from the earth's gravitational field and come back down in another country—impressive, aggressive and most definitely a GUY THING. Von Braun's expertise gave the world ballistic missiles and the Saturn V boosters that helped power the Apollo missions to the moon.

After digging into the history of the Everest expeditions, oceanography, hydraulics, the NASA moon shots and NASCAR, I was starting to think my wife was right all along. Except the other night while we were enjoying some incredible homemade lasagna (the best I've ever had—Marcus Aurelius would be proud) it occurred to me that while necessity is the mother of invention, the mothers of inventors, and sisters and daughters, have all benefitted from the male compulsion to discover stuff. The first hand-crank pasta machine, for example, patented in 1906 by Angelo Vitantonio, an Italian immigrant living in Cleveland, stands as a cast aluminum tribute to these "guy things" we do. Who can take an honest look in the mirror (also invented by a guy—you're welcome, ladies) and say their life is not significantly better due to the universal law of noodle uniformity?

It's stellar research like this that tells me I'm on the right track. To pull up lame at this point is not an option. My wife, whether she knows it or not, and my daughters, regardless of whether they choose careers in environmental biology or cosmetology, will be impacted by my willingness to hang out on the slippery slope for as long as it takes to sort this mess out.

7

MORNING AT THE MUSEUM

G rant Keddie digs for bones. He also investigates fossil finds and a variety of other West Coast artifacts brought to his attention. This is the kind of gig you get after several productive years at university kicking around the archaeology department. I was first introduced to Keddie's work when I read a newspaper article about a woolly mammoth graveyard on Vancouver Island, of all places. The evidence, now property of the Royal BC Museum, appears to be the remains of several mammoths. Most of these relics have been unearthed on the Saanich peninsula, about a half hour drive from my mother-in-law's condo in Victoria.

While I no longer considered myself a hard-nosed "young earth" creationist, I was, nevertheless, suspicious of a scenario that included prehistoric elephant bones, gravel deposits and Vancouver Island. Not only were these mammoths (cousins to the modern day Asian elephant) a long way from home, they apparently got lost about thirteen thousand years before Noah's behemoths trudged down the gangplank of the ark and off into the post-flood sunset. To anyone raised with a creationist worldview, scenarios such as these can be problematic. I was hoping that a mammoth expert could straighten me out, so I contacted Keddie, who is the Curator of Archaeology at the Royal BC Museum, and set up an interview.

A few mornings later I bounded up the concrete steps into the museum courtyard, backpack and camera slung over my shoulder. I was giddy with nervous energy and cafe mocha, and unsure that I would be able to carry my end of an archaeological discourse with a museum curator. I took a deep breath and relaxed once I realized that I wasn't the only person heading into foreign territory. Grant Keddie was about to come face to face with one of the few creationists that he'd unearthed in his thirty-some years on the job.

After being checked through security I arrived at a sign-in desk manned by a museum staffer named Dave. Since I'd never been 'backstage' at a museum before, I thought I'd warm up on Dave, and find out what he did. He told me how he spent his mornings sorting through email, and mentioned that earlier that morning he'd fielded questions about a bald eagle discovered in a freezer at the north end of the island. Before Dave was able to dive in to the chilling details, a guy in khakis and a chartreuse button-down shirt rounded the corner and marched into the lobby. It was Grant Keddie.

We shook hands and he quickly escorted me into a small elevator and down into the basement of the museum complex. I followed silently as he glided through a maze of rooms overflowing with pale cabinets and bathed in cold white light. An endless string of fluorescent tubes clung to the ceiling like grubs to the underside of a backyard paving stone. We slipped through a series of military grey doors, squeezing past too many cabinets (and too few humans) before we arrived at his office.

I settled into a black plastic chair, the only bare surface in the room apart from the slide of an old microscope perched to the right of his computer keyboard. A message—PROPERTY OF GRANT KEDDIE— scrawled on duct tape and slapped on the side of the microscope reminded me of high school chemistry class. The aboriginal jewelry hanging from his neck reminded me of Mr. Taylor, my old chemistry teacher. Hopefully the next few minutes held more promise than those five wasted months back in ninth grade.

Before I managed to pull out a voice recorder or even ask my first question, Keddie was going full throttle, speaking with an unexpected air of excitement. For the next ninety minutes I was an audience of one for an archaeologist thrilled with his career and passionate about sharing his take on everything from historical climate change in the Pacific Northwest to the latest developments in human genetics and how scientists hope to eradicate disease once they understand the trillions of microbes that make their home inside the human body.

"Trillions? Really?" I blurted out when he stopped to take a breath.

"Absolutely," he responded. "Just remember that we are not a single organism, we are a "symbion." We have over three pounds of bacteria in our intestinal tract, we have bacteria in our hair and our eyes, all over our body… thousands and thousands of individual species—and we cannot exist without them. They are part of who we are. If you added up the total number of cells of the whole organism of which we are part, only about ten percent of those are human. Ninety percent of our cells are actually bacteria and viruses. The big question is 'What is this system all about?' It's mind boggling when you think about it."

Factoids and anecdotes burst out of him with all the ragged randomness of the papers and journals piled on the file cabinets around the perimeter of his office. Eventually, I did manage to steer our conversation towards some of the more elementary controversies surrounding the evolution-creation debate.

"How often is it that you get something carbon dated and find an artifact or fossil that is out of sequence with the surrounding strata?" I asked.

"Well," he paused for a moment. "The only time that ever happens is when you're dealing with sites that are less than 2,000 years old. You might have ten dates at a site and find that the uppermost layer is off. Sometimes the upper layers get disturbed by tree roots." He continued, "But you can't trust the dates that another archaeologist came up with thirty years ago. You build on what they've done, but you have to be very critical of their research and your own."

"There have been huge advances in radiometric dating in the last few decades," Keddie told me, "but it's only good up to 50,000 years. The trick is to get as many dates as you can—the artifact you're after, the surrounding soil, pollen—all of these things are indicators. Yes, it costs money, and some people might take shortcuts and can't be bothered. There's the trade-off of paying your own staff to do the carbon dating versus contracting out. That's what we do here at the museum."

"So do most teams do their own carbon dating?" I asked, suddenly aware how little I knew about this oft-maligned technology.

"In the old days, yes, universities had students covering that, but sometimes they were more concerned with completing their thesis than doing the work properly. Today we have companies that focus exclusively on carbon-dating artifacts from all over the world. We use a company in Florida. If there's something that doesn't fit, I can contact the lab and say, "I'm pretty confident that this artifact is, say, 800 years old—and your data isn't cutting it." Once in a while we discover that someone wasn't doing their job, but usually we catch these things. Remember, none of these discoveries happen chronologically. So every piece of information either challenges a previous record or confirms and fits in with already known data. Again the rule is: the more dates you get, the better you understand the sequence."

"Tell me about these mammoths," I asked. "How did they end up here?"

"The fact that we found a lot of mammoths and mastodons doesn't tell us that this is an extra-ordinary place for them. It only tells us that geologically they happened to be covered up by glacial sediments. About 11,200 years ago, the sea level was quite different—many of the San Juan Islands in Washington State were almost joined together by land bridges. We've also found human settlements dating back about 4,200 years. They won't be the oldest, but because of changes to the shoreline they're the oldest we've found around here. But in Oregon we have dated the DNA found in human excrement so we know that humans have been in the vicinity for over 14,000 years. But you probably want to go downstairs and see some mammoth bones, am I right?"

Nice segue, I thought, as we headed out of his office and back to the elevator.

8

BUILDING ON SAND

The next morning, after a half hour drive north of Victoria, I arrived at a sunny beach. I tied up the laces on my hiking boots and turned south into a salty wind. Grant Keddie had mentioned that as long as the tide was at low point, I'd be able to walk far enough to see the glacial layers in the cliff side and just maybe, if I was lucky, a mammoth fossil.

After setting off like an overstuffed Sherpa under the midday sun, I quickly decided that shedding a couple layers might keep me from expiring right there on the sand. The distant cliffs appeared no closer than when I had started out. I glanced at my watch. Ten minutes had passed. This was going to be harder than advertised. The constant shifting of sand under my feet made for slow progress. I kept my eyes down, focusing on where my next step would take me.

How many stragglers had wandered this beach, never looking up at the cliffs where the fossil remains of a community of mammoths lay entombed? How many never even bothered to look past their own bootlaces for things unusual? I stopped and looked down between my feet to where a piece of vertebra, parched and yellowing, lay half covered in sand. I picked it up, held it aloft and stared through the cavity where the spinal cord would have been, out into the calm blue waters of the Salish Sea. This bone fragment likely belonged to a sea lion. I tucked it into my camera case and kept walking.

There's a story that Jesus tells in the Gospel of Luke about two builders who went about their construction projects in two very different ways. The first builder secured a piece of property to build a house. He dug down deep until he hit bedrock and then proceeded to lay a foundation and build his house. The second builder found a similar piece of property, but never bothered digging down to the bedrock. Luke doesn't tell us, but it's likely that this builder would have had some knowledge of local weather patterns. Why didn't he dig deeper? When Jesus told the story, he emphasized that the foolish builder didn't listen to the advice given him and threw together a shack without a firm foundation. Jesus said he didn't obey, didn't take the necessary steps to merge what he knew to be consistent with reality, and design his house with those realities in mind. The wise builder, on the other hand, knew that even if he lost his house in the storm, he still had the rock. He could build again. But he wasn't going to put his faith in the shifting sand.

I didn't have any intentions of replacing God as my foundation, but it was unsettling to ponder whether my creationist worldview was perched on shifting sand or solid rock. As I trudged south along that beach on Vancouver Island, I wrestled with the fear that my life of faith was becoming unglued. Not completely, but enough. I was being exposed to a cascade of new information that appeared to contradict some foundational biblical truths that I'd spent my life holding tightly to.

Eventually I found myself standing with the Pacific waves at my back, staring up at the face of Grant Keddie's mammoth cliff. Even though I had no formal geological training, I had a hunch that this particular wall of earth and marine deposits was not intent on remaining a cliff for very much longer. I spotted an inconsequential trickle of sand and gravel deposits about half way up the cliff face—thirty-five feet above my perch on a giant piece of driftwood. It was as if the wall of glacial sediment rising above me to the view homes on the ledge above had sprung a leak. A dirt leak. As I surveyed the face of the cliff, I noticed that the earth was pouring out of this unlikely dam in several places.

I have been lulled to sleep by the patter of raindrops on my tent. I've been pulled violently from a dream by hurricane winds pounding against my bedroom window. But I'd never sat still long enough to listen while the earth babbled. It was imperceptible at first, but I could actually hear it. And it sounded remarkably like rain. After a few seconds my senses had become so attuned to the gentle cascade of the sand above me that I could no longer hear the Pacific Ocean behind me, roaring its own song to the creator.

Perhaps I should have backed away from those shifting sands. It was entirely possible that today would be the day a lethal landslide on Vancouver Island crashed onto the news and a father of two was nominated for a Darwin Award. But I didn't move. I'd never felt so at home in the face of the slippery slope. I stood there, a silent witness to the transience of nature. I didn't bother to look at the silly timepiece on my wrist. It didn't matter at what rate time was passing in the world of humans. For this moment, I was transfixed by the dropping of the sands in God's own hourglass.

I don't expect that this cliff will be here centuries from now. As surely as this earth orbits the sun, the ocean will rise again, like it has so many times before, and lay down another layer of dark, crustacean-enriched sediment over this beach. And then one day, long after my body has ceased being a soul bucket, someone else will wander along this beach, beneath these cliffs. And they'll stop to stare up the dark ocean floor exposed layer by layer in the side of this island. And just maybe, if they can manage to tune out the roar of the Pacific Ocean they might be able to listen to the earth.

CALVIN WRAY

9

TROUBLE IN PARADISE

everal months had passed since I first asked my musician friend Dan for his perspective on Genesis. I had believed there were only two possible answers—young earth creationism or old earth Intelligent Design. And here I was still sorting through the wreckage of that conversation, trying to drag a few threads of sense out of a tangled mess of discontent. There's this thing that happens when you start looking at your own version of the way things are. You wonder if adopting a brand new way of filtering and deciphering life might bring a different result. You're doing everything right, thinking the right thoughts, even demonstrating an impressive array of proper behaviors, but you find the results distasteful and far less than satisfying. This is where I found myself now.

The feeling reminds me of the time we went to this really expensive Asian restaurant in downtown Vancouver, and I had a chance for the first time in years to enjoy an authentic Chinese meal (unless you consider the number three combo at Sweet and Sour Dynasty in the food court authentic). I'm a seafood lover through and through: salmon, shrimp, halibut, lobster, mussels and squid. If it has gills or pinchers and a shell and lives in the ocean or even has beachfront property I'm going to inhale it.

(My dad used to take me fishing as a youngster. I think we caught the odd salmon, but those early morning excursions were more exercises in boat rental protocol than actual hunter/gatherer expeditions. If natural selection acted upon fishermen based on their ability to locate the catch of the day, you would have found the Wray family fossils in some southern Vancouver Island tidal pool, covered in silt and entombed in soggy, orange life-jackets caked in Cheerios and stuffed with cat hair.)

On this particular day, my birthday, I was sitting with my family and my parents in one of the fanciest Chinese eateries in the whole city. We had ordered a variety of dishes and sat back to enjoy the meal, which began arriving one course at a time within only minutes. The spicy squid was a winner, but I was puzzled at my complete disappointment with the prawns. More puzzling still was the fact that my six-year-old daughter was happily dissecting her prawns right next to me. Six-year-olds usually don't like any restaurant entree that doesn't include both chicken and nuggets. I had expected this prawn encounter to be a straightforward affair. One simply has to pick up the beast, pull with both hands until the tail separates from the body cavity and then take a bite. It is also wise to interject guttural sounds like "MMMM-mm" and "Oh... Oh... good" to let the other members of your tribe know that you are indeed enjoying the feast and don't care if the pork lettuce wrap ever arrives.

From my first bite I suspected there must be something wrong with these prawns but my stubbornness wouldn't allow me to disavow them as a delicacy. I would need to try harder. Perhaps prawns were an acquired taste, like steak tartar or badger tongue.

I was tempted to call the waiter over and explain with all the Christian charity I could muster between gags that this fine establishment was mistaken if they thought they could serve twenty-three dollar menu items that tasted like rancid guacamole and get away with it. So I tried again. And again. After several failed attempts, in a rare moment of humility, I asked my wife, who knows all things cuisine, how she was enjoying her prawns. She looked at me, glanced down at the carnage on my plate, and without skipping a beat as she reached for a platter of Peking Duck, said, "You're eating the wrong end."

§

Growing up in a conservative Christian household isn't something you try to do. It's like growing up with six toes on your left foot. It just happens, you meet life on your terms, and try not to hurt yourself on the coffee table. I was well into my young adult years before I had even thought of categorizing my take on human origins, and at this point it had only been a few months that my eyes had been opened to the possibility of alternative Genesis interpretations. I now understand what makes a conservative evangelical a conservative evangelical. We fear change. It's a documented fact. And it's genetic. We fear change in government, change in freeway signage, change in the organic smoothie menu at the drive-thru, and more than anything else, we fear change when it comes to interpreting our faith.

In 1654, a similarly conservative Irish Archbishop named James Usher used the genealogy in Genesis to determine that the earth was created on Sunday, October 23, 4004 BC, but that the creation process started the previous day at sundown.

With the age of the earth determined to be around six thousand years, it became necessary to articulate the doctrine of catastrophism—a geological model that holds that the earth was shaped by series of giant disasters, all within this six thousand year span. But then in 1785, James Hutton, the father of geology, published *Theory of the Earth*. Hutton observed that Hadrian's Wall, which had been built by the Romans fifteen hundred years earlier, was showing virtually no signs of change. He suspected that the processes needed to shape the earth would require more time than has previously been allotted by theologians. Let the games begin.

Young earth creationists (YEC) believe that we humans appeared on earth in our present form about 6,000 years ago. They believe that Adam and Eve were the first humans, and maintain that any fossil evidence in existence is the result of a worldwide flood that happened within the last four thousand years. Recent studies in the U.S. show that close to 60% of the population hold to a creationist perspective in one form or another. In Canada, the percentage appears to be slightly lower, but only because a lot of people wouldn't complete the survey because there was a hockey game on TV.

But young earth creationists, it turns out, aren't the only kind of creationists on the block. Some creationists, affectionately referred to as old-earthers (or as the young-earthers like to call them, 'heretics') do allow for vast amounts of time to be inserted into Genesis Chapter One so that the tens of millions of years proposed by geologists don't have to be discounted outright. One school of thought referred to as the Day–Age model suggests that each DAY in the six-day creation week is actually describing a phase of creative process rather than an actual twenty-four hour day. And then there's the Gap theory, which states that between Genesis 1:1 and 1:2, God did a whole lot of experimenting. The Gap theory shouldn't be confused with the 'God of the Gaps,' which refers to our tendency to suggest divine action as an explanation for any physical phenomenon that we can't explain in physical terms. (Just last week at the outlet mall I walked right past "The Gap." It was sandwiched between Fossil Jeans and Build-a-Bear. I suspect that this bizarre juxtaposition would have escaped my notice were it not for my current state of mind.)

While I couldn't call myself a hard-line young earth creationist, I wasn't really predisposed to one of these theories over the other. But I knew that whichever interpretation of Genesis I settled on would be a reflection of the respect I awarded the scientific community.

The Big Bang theory, for example, is seen by some creationists as anti-biblical, as it attempts to demonstrate what happened in the beginning—without God. And they assert that because it's only a 'theory' then it's not worth its own weight in quarks and leptons. I'm fine with the Big Bang. In fact many believers have reconciled this instance of cosmic inspiration with those seven words in Genesis, "And God said 'let there be light.'"

BANG!!

The problem with accepting the Big Bang is that you pretty much have to accept the chronology that goes along with it. Which, in turn, leaves you with a lot more gaps and holes to insert into your reading of Genesis chapter one. And we haven't even landed on chapter two yet, where things get even more complicated.

"Then the Lord God formed a man from the dust of the ground." (Gen 2:7)

I stopped cold one morning, backed up and read it again. And then I gave it another pass, this time more slowly, as if by doing so I could will the text to read something a little more like, "And the Lord God created man in an instant about six thousand years ago from the dust of the ground."

The funny thing was, I had always been comfortable allowing the phrase, "And God said, 'Let there be light'" to incorporate everything that exists in the material universe: space, time, energy, atoms, molecules, the laws of thermodynamics, beets. Now I was being tempted to stretch the boundaries further. I found myself contemplating an unexpected scenario. Was it conceivable that "And the Lord God created man from the dust of the ground" might just encompass the entire spectrum of the evolutionary understanding of human origins?

Naaaw! Just keep reading.

I had been thinking the same thoughts, answering the questions the same old way, and yet I was feeling less and less satisfied with the answers. My personal statement of faith had become distasteful even to myself. If there was the slightest possibility that I was getting any of this wrong, well… I heard a still small voice utter those familiar words that I'd first heard in Chinatown: "You're eating the wrong end."

Obviously, the book of Genesis was going to need some serious attention on my part. Not because I didn't know how it read, but because for the first time, I wasn't sure what it meant. Where was I supposed to begin in this "book of beginnings"? For several months I had been carrying a secret, a gnawing sensation in my gut that everything I claimed to know about how humans had come to inhabit this planet was suspect.

And then it happened in an instant.

In one moment I had drawn air into my lungs as a life long proponent of a literal Genesis creation paradigm, and the next moment I exhaled a glorious blast of "I don't know anything for sure anymore!" I sat for a moment and pondered. I pinched myself. I hadn't been swallowed up in doubt like Charles Darwin. I didn't curse God and die, as suggested by Job's wife. In fact, I didn't feel the slightest weight of depression. I just felt a wonderful sense of freedom; freedom from the pressure of having to regurgitate answers that I couldn't sell anymore. To unbelieving friends. To myself.

For years I'd been living under the pressure to justify my "Christian" version of origins, even though there was almost no evidence that the scientific establishment would consider, and none that my friends who weren't Christians would believe for a minute. And all the while that other universe, the one in all the science magazines—the universe that Hawking and Einstein and Sagan and Darwin wrote about with very little reference to Scripture—seemed to be ticking along without any trouble.

Until this moment, I'd never considered that any of these so-called experts might actually be getting it right. Until this moment I'd been on a polite little hike into some unfamiliar corners of my faith, where I was certain I'd survey the landscape, engage in polite dinner conversation with a few anti-God types, pick up a Darwin T-shirt at the gift shop and be home in time for Letterman. I wasn't prepared for uncertainty. I didn't even know how to stand up properly in a room where I didn't have all the answers.

What a rare and beautiful thing it is to have an epiphany, to be swept up in the glorious rapture of unbridled 'not knowing.' This flavour of not knowing was ripe and juicy and tear-inducing and unexpectedly joyous, like the first time you taste strawberries dipped in balsamic vinegar. This was simple ignorance in its purest form. I didn't know everything.

I didn't have to know everything.

10

THE HALF LIFE OF PORK

I t was a Sunday like any other Sunday when the worship pastor cornered me in the sound booth, interrupting those seven peaceful minutes that divide the end of sound check from the start of the service.

"Hey... can we get together for lunch sometime this week?" he asked me.

"Sure," I answered back, not knowing the reason for the meeting, but always on the lookout for a free meal. Cory had become a good friend over the past three years since we'd been attending North Langley Community Church. The instant connection was music but the friendship had grown from there.

"I want to talk with you about your book," he said.

"Oh... kay," I said nervously. "It's not really a book yet. It's a post-it note. Do I need to bring anything with me?"

"Nope, we're just going to talk. But I need a ride."

"I'll pick you up here at the church at noon," I replied. Even though it was only a short conversation, my mind set off at breakneck pace trying to surmise why he wanted to meet. On the outside I remained calm and focused on my task of maintaining a decent audio mix for the musicians on stage. But I could barely hear the band over the noise in my head. I was penciled in for one of two conversations. Either Cory wanted to tell me that he was excited about the direction of my writing, or I was in for a rough ninety minutes of lunchtime grilling. Perhaps he had good news. Maybe he had reconnected with a friend from college who had risen to prominence in a successful publishing company, and had become ecstatic when he learned of my brave project and wanted to meet me.

A more likely scenario was that a posse of powerful Mennonite church elders sequestered in a chamber decorated in ornate velvet curtains and gigantic frescoes on the ceiling depicting farmer sausage had held some secret elections, and they had decided that my friend Cory would have to take one for the team. They were sending him in to shut me up!

It was also possible the official Mennonite "Ministry of Creative Arts and Funky Projects We'd Love to Fund" had gotten wind of my idea to toss biblical creationism under the Sunday school bus, recognized the brilliance of my plan, and were offering positive reinforcement in the form of a six figure advance. Or they were going to pay for my silence. And I had even been asked to pilot the wagon to my own execution. Perhaps I was over-reacting.

When I got home from church, I told Arlene about my Monday appointment.

"They think you're a heretic!" she blurted out.

"I think you're right," I said. "Are there any other churches nearby, where we can lay low for a while? At least until I get the manuscript into safe hands?" I was more than worried until I remembered one of the great rules of writing: Conflict equals drama.

"I'm going to record our conversation," I said triumphantly. "This is exactly the break I've been looking for. It'll push the plot forward."

Twenty-three hours later I found myself sitting on an unforgiving plywood chair against the wall of a Chinese food eatery. In front of me, a platter piled high with noodles, steamed vegetables and a healthy dose of atomic red sweet and sour looked tempting. The tiny sign taped to the glass over the buffet stated clearly that it was pork. My newly acquired skill of not believing everything I read made me skeptical.

Unable to withstand the suspense any longer, I decided to break the ice.

"So Cory... am I busted? Did the church elders send you to "clean up this mess?"

"Yeah... exactly" he said stone faced, and then broke into a smile.

"Nope. No worries. I'm just really intrigued by what you're getting yourself into. How's it coming along?"

"Well, as of today, I'm not exactly where I thought I'd end up... I originally got into this to get a better idea of how atheists viewed the world."

Cory was shoveling combo #4 with a tiny plastic fork, and showed no signs of letting up. I eyed my own plate and decided to keep talking. It wouldn't hurt to let whatever it was on my plate lose some of its caustic orange glow. What's the half-life of pork?

"So, I wake up this morning and I realize that I've barely begun to understand how massive God really is." I put down my fork and stretched out an imaginary canvas with my hands. "It's like I have always considered God as being this wide." My index fingers hovered, almost touching above the table. "And God is really this wide." My hands separated dramatically like the blue angels on a flyby to the outer reaches of the table. "The way I see things now, even if I could quadruple my bandwidth, God's perspective is so much wider than I'll ever be able to grasp..." and I kept talking until his plate was empty.

"It's all about loss of control." Cory started up. It was my turn to eat."When our world is tidy, it's easy to maintain control. To keep everything in a box and have all the answers."

"I didn't start out wanting to have ALL the answers," I said, with my mouth still full of pretend chow mein.

"What do you mean?"

I swallowed. "I didn't begin this journey trying to prove anything, really. I simply wanted to know how an atheist could survive intellectually with evolution... So I'd have a better understanding of how they think, what makes them tick. I know that God created everything but I wanted to investigate their manifesto on my own terms, and maybe find a rebuttal."

"But when you start coming up with answers that some people don't like your mind starts playing tricks on you. Is that it?"

"All I know is that none of this is going where I had expected."

"Where did you think it was going?" he asked.

"I guess I was planning on all of the unknowns being more clinical, you know—more of an intellectual exercise. I wasn't expecting it all to be so... so unsettling."

After we'd finished lunch and I dropped Cory back at the church, I reached into the backseat for a notebook that had traveled with me for several months. I flipped pages until I arrived at THE LIST—a page full of questions that I'd been pondering. Two lists, actually. List A was a collection of topics I still needed to research. Like how had Charles Darwin managed to maintain his status as the golden child of the scientific community for the last 150 years? Was academia secretly conspiring against Christians by propping up a theory that had run its course and collapsed under its own weight? Can the theory of evolution be rationally explained within the pages of Genesis? Why would the British Royal Navy name a sailing ship "HMS Beagle"—after dogs that, more often than not, detest water?

I continued flipping until I found another set of questions. List B was a collection of questions much less concerned about the physical evidence of a Creator's methods. List B is a set of internal thoughts about God and this journey. I read it again.

1. Is it possible to get so confused in this journey that I will be unwilling to climb back to my original position as a Bible-based creationist?

2. Am I convinced that God will search for me in times of doubt, if I lose my way?

3. What if my current interpretation of Genesis is totally screwed up? (I don't want to talk about it.)

4. Is my belief in the Bible stronger than my belief in the God of the Bible?

Was I afraid that I might come across a body of evidence—or even a shred of it—compelling enough to destabilize my faith? Was there a scenario in which my God hypothesis didn't win the day? What would it take to shake my faith? Or blast it to bits?

I reached for a pen and scribbled another question on list B.

Is it possible to go down this road and not make enemies?

§

From the first days of this investigation, I had been convinced that a safe, clinical tour of the evolutionist worldview would be both invigorating and a stretching experience—good for my faith. At least that's what I kept telling myself. As the days turned over, however, it became clear to me as I wandered up and down some very old questions, sometimes stopping to catch my breath and other times picking myself up to wipe off the dirt, that this slippery slope is where a lot of people spend their entire lives.

Even though belief in God had been a constant in my life since before I could remember, I had never considered what people without any formalized beliefs about God or the universe thought about when they did. I was sure they were a lot like me, except they never had to drag six months of church bulletins out from under the driver's seat. Relative truth might be a popular notion, but I was getting my first taste of the restlessness that comes with being anything less than sure. It felt a little like drowning and a lot like trying to fly in a bad dream. I had lived my entire Christian life in a sheltered land, an out of the way place, unaware that this seemingly sure foundation of faith might also be susceptible to its own cataclysm. A sudden, violent shift in plate tectonics could easily trigger a private theological tsunami if I didn't dare dig a little deeper, and learn to give reasons for my faith, not reasons why my faith was immune to reason.

I knew that unless I was willing to walk into the long, cold shadows that haunted this valley I would never truly understand. I would only believe. And I needed to know the difference.

11

FLASHLIGHTS AND DARWIN

I f I was going to accomplish anything in my search to understand these atheists and their crush on evolutionary theory, it was mandatory that I show some respect for my adversary. I knew almost nothing about Charles Darwin beyond the fact that he could lay claim to one of the largest fan clubs on the planet. And that was just counting all the unemployed zoology majors. I didn't know how his five-year stint as a naturalist aboard the HMS Beagle had started him on journey to disprove the existence of God. I didn't know why Darwin's theory of natural selection was still held in such high regard after 150 years of scientific advancement. My first task would be to read *On the Origin of Species*.

The problem was, I didn't know any Christians that would admit to harboring a copy of Darwin's book in their library. I'd have to head to a bookstore. Better take cash to avoid a paper trail. And then there was the tiny matter of sneaking this piece of biology propaganda into the house where I'd be forced to read it by flashlight under the covers late at night. I had attempted similar acts of bravado with *Mad Magazine* growing up and had gotten away with it. However, this time the degree of risk would be much higher due to the fact that my wife can't sleep when there's someone lying next to her under the covers with a flashlight. And I'd have to protect myself—my soul. Maybe I could just scan a few pages every day, and then take a hot shower to avoid getting muddied in a wave of abject hopelessness. And I'd take some notes. Get in, get out, nobody gets hurt.

The trick, as far as I could figure it, was to find answers to some nagging questions without turning into a raving atheist. The only thing I knew with any certainty was that God already knew the whole story and wasn't going to be caught off guard by an angry British biologist (the first in a long line). As certain as I was of the silliness of the whole evolutionary proposition, I was even more sure that God wasn't sitting on the stairs at Harvard or MIT waiting nervously for the latest results from the lab. God knew very well how I had managed to arrive at this juncture in history. "The truth is the truth is the truth," I repeated nervously as I headed off in search of a decent flashlight.

12

THE SHED

’m having one of those days again. I don't know much about depression, but I am restless under the weight of a dark malaise that has settled over me like the clouds on another rainy weekend in February. It's cold season. It's getting close to tax time. Perhaps I am worn out by all the information I've ingested, but I think it goes deeper than that. I think there is more to my discontent than the pondering that accompanies the usual questions about geology or natural selection.

What if I'm losing my way in this process of finding? What if I'm drifting in imperceptible, glacial proportions away from where I want to end up? What if by my pondering of all this science, the pushing and prodding, stretching and twisting, dissecting and micro-analyzing, that I discover as the famous saying goes "... that the theologians have been there all along." Am I really going to inspire anyone to greater faith by this exercise in reason?

Last weekend my parents dropped in for dinner. I made the phone call and Arlene did the cooking. She would have phoned, but that would've left me with nothing to do. My dad and I picked up where we'd left off three weeks earlier. I had just finished *Only a Theory*, by Kenneth R. Miller, and my dad was on his second go-round of *Scandal of the Evangelical Mind* by Mark Noll. This time he's writing in the margins. I can tell that my mom is not in the least bit impressed with my fascination with all this origins nonsense.

"I think you're obsessive-compulsive," she said matter-of-factly, as I began showing off my latest purchases. I had hauled a dozen never read masterpieces out of a dingy, glorious used bookstore on the main street of Port Townsend, Washington—a veritable treasure chest of scientific thought.

"Obsessive? Compulsive?" Why is it obsessive-compulsive if my brain doesn't have an off-switch right now?"

"You're in too deep," she said.

"These are not the delusional ramblings from the back forty of an addled brain. I can't lie around the backyard planning my new deck, when I should be trying to figure out a way to tell YOUR grandchildren that the story of Noah's Ark, as they were taught it in Sunday school, never happened!"

I was waiting for her to pull out her classic line, something about "moderation in all things." I would be ready for her this time. I'd been prepping since the last time she used that line after she heard I'd biked ninety-five kilometers in the rain to prove I could, and then spent the next four days walking like I had rickets. I would be waiting with my Thomas Edison anecdote, the one where he responded to a reporter who had asked him what it was like to fail at something 1,000 times. According to the yarn, Edison replied, "I have not failed one thousand times. I have successfully discovered one thousand ways to NOT make a light bulb!" This, I had convinced myself, would end the controversy. I would follow that up with "Everyone knows that nothing great in life is ever accomplished by attempting anything in moderation." I'd been rehearsing this, and it would flow effortlessly off the end of my tongue. Dead simple and stunning—absolutely true.

Instead, my mom, who usually lobs high arcing slow pitches, came with the heat. "I think it all comes back to our connection with Jesus. Isn't that why we're here for our seventy years, if we're lucky? We can't get caught up with all of these other things. My faith is never going to be shaken if I have a real, growing connection with Jesus. Everything comes back to Jesus."

Didn't see that one coming.

"No, it doesn't," I fired back, suddenly aware that I could be struck dead at any moment. My mom doesn't have a temper, but she does have some serious pull. Just ask the people in her prayer circle.

I fumbled for context, stood and pointed to the utility shed sitting smartly against the early evening sky in the back corner of our yard. I felt like Charlton Heston staring down the Red Sea. "That shed behind you, next to the emerald cedars, isn't about Jesus. Well, it could be about Jesus, but only if I built it properly. Okay, perhaps it's possible that by adhering to classic architectural lines, solid construction and craftsmanship, that mere shed could give glory to God. But only as a result of truth in building practices."

My mom said nothing, so I kept going.

"Building that shed is about math, and understanding building materials, structural practices, and nails, and, and geometry so the snow slides off and kills the hydrangeas instead of the cat. What about quality of workmanship? I can only build that shed in glory to God if I follow the rules of the natural laws that are already laid out. Either that or I do my best and it falls down and we all laugh because I'm like four years old, and didn't know any better."

I was just getting started.

"The wood has to be this thick." I sliced the cool evening air between us as I drew imaginary two by four studs with my fingers. "And the concrete slab has to cure, what about the slab! WHAT ABOUT THE SLAB? If I have free access to the instructions that will help me to mix the concrete correctly and I ignore that advice, how is that glorifying to God? Does it matter if I mock the intricate dance of limestone and clay, burning together at 1600 degrees centigrade to form cement binder molecules? Maybe I should toss in some Nutella just to be sure? Did you consider geometry and the classic Greek architectural principles that I might have employed which would have caused passersby to stare in awe and glorify their Father in heaven? Sure, Jesus could have built a better shed, and done it faster. Because he's a carpenter!

"It didn't have anything to do with Jesus," I said almost apologetically. "Building that stupid shed was about building that stupid shed! The resulting creation can be about Jesus, my motivation can be about Jesus, but the shed has to be built in this universe using local gravity, and molecules and lumber sized according to a historical understanding of how much stress it can take before it snaps off like a…" My voice trailed off. I had run out of words. And gas.

Obsessive? Compulsive? Where does she get that idea?

13

WENDEL'S DOWN ON THE FRASER

The welcome noise of loose rocks under wheels marks my arrival at my favorite parking spot, next to the old railway station in Fort Langley. Whenever I need to just sit and ponder, I make the fifteen minute drive from home to this little town beyond the suburbs. Being a city boy, Fort Langley is the only real town in my short list of places to go.

On the coldest, soggiest nights when the Fraser River is blanketed in fog—a fog that rolls through the lonesome streets, bouncing off darkened store windows, swirling in lazy circles around shadowy stop signs and silver tree branches before floating off in search of another obstacle to flirt with—I like to curl up by myself on the dark, blustery patio tucked tight under a sign that reads Wendel's Cafe and Bookstore.

Inside, Wendel's is warm and alive. Steaming Americanos energize and the room simmers with busy chatter of college students and suburban desperados, all of them on the lam from the pace of the city. Tonight is "Pasta Night," and if I wasn't still full from dinner I'd be tempted to settle over a well-worn table next to the window and chew on a lasagna.

Most nights I arrive well layered and well fed, so I only need a coffee and a brownie to keep me company at a small table outside. But I'm not alone here. Wendel's is the place I come to sort myself out or find God. Nothing traumatizing like the apostle Paul's Damascus road encounter mind you, but I know that God is here, mostly because at Wendel's, I stop long enough to listen. Some nights I'm tempted to loiter among the books in the tiny aisles inside the store and listen to the groaning of the floorboards while I peruse the spines and dust jackets of books I don't yet own. (After a while you can tell where you are in the store by the sound of the floor. You know you're a regular at Wendel's when as you're thumbing through one book and shuffling along the row, you get distracted by a particular groan underfoot, and you know that if you glance to your left, at about shoulder height, you'll see something by Deepak Chopra.) But mostly I sit out on the deck. Being outside, even in the bleakest weather, keeps me away from the conversations on the other side, the cozy side of the walls, and I can bury my face in a book or a journal, while toasting nicely under the crackle of a thirty foot long propane heater suspended from the dark wooden soffits.

Sometimes God shows up when I write. Sometimes I think I hear him in the whooshing of tires as they slosh along the main street of this town. It's not that I'm confusing God with any of these mere physical objects. I know he's not IN the tires in the all-terrain, steel-belted pantheistic sense. But in the sense that he holds the entire universe together by his very word, I know for sure that he is out and about tonight, keeping motorists safe. (And I could sell a lot of tires if I could just find the right way to market this.)

Some nights when I'm at Wendel's I imagine him rolling off the cold floor of an empty boxcar as the train strolls through, dressed like a hobo, but with Jim Cavezeil eyes. I tell myself I'd recognize God if he showed up here one night. He could do it.

Tonight I had planned on writing about Wendel's. I want to turn Wendell into an actual character, a front porch sage of sorts, an ever-silent friend. But instead of launching into a muddled essay on my mute, caffeine-dispensing mentor, I saw God. Well I didn't actually see him. I saw hints of him in the blinking green traffic light that dangled over the pedestrian crosswalk not twenty yards from my perch on the sporadically heated, mostly vacant patio deck.

As the green light flickered off and on rhythmically, my gaze fell onto the black, wet asphalt in the intersection, and I was captivated by the green hue that pulsed across the puddles. The puddles weren't the source of the green light, but they were oscillating in perfect time, reflecting as accurately as they were able the hues from the traffic light above.

I turned away so I could focus on the task at hand, my writing, but as I peered through the cafe windows to the magazine rack stacked high with *Cosmo* and *Quilting Monthly*, I couldn't escape that pervasive green light. The window panes between me and the magazine rack were shimmering in perfect time to that green light. Even when I was looking in the wrong direction, I couldn't escape the unfaltering patient luminescence of that traffic light.

And then I thought I heard God say, "If you knew me better, you'd know that I don't hide myself from anyone. It's not who I am." I didn't look around to find a source of the voice. I knew there wasn't any audible voice. Just the unmistakable clarity that comes when you are all alone and you're not trying to think or say anything and yet someone else has suddenly started a whole new conversation and they are way smarter than you. I turned back from the window, over to the flashing green puddle, and then up to the traffic light. I kept staring and wondered if I'd be asked to take my shoes off. I kept listening and heard nothing but the gravelly grinding of the overhead heater. It sputtered and stopped and for a few seconds sounded more like a tub of Jiffy Pop after you take it off the stove. Silence.

Then I thought I heard God say, "Do you remember what love feels like when you first find it? Do you remember that giddy state of mind or heart that makes you feel more awake and healthy than when you could sleep and you could eat, but you can't anymore because you're in love—do you remember that? Well, I invented that feeling. But I never lose it over time. Time doesn't work on me. Can you even imagine how much I enjoy being found by those who are searching for me? Even when they're facing the wrong way or staring down at a puddle or at the cover of *Cosmo*? Even if they're not sure I exist. Even if they've never read a single word from a single page of any of my best selling authors? Anyone who really wants to will see me in the details of my other book—the book of nature."

And then I thought I heard God say that trying to turn Wendell into a character was a cool idea. Just don't expect more from him than fresh coffee, killer brownies and the occasional lasagna.

And then I didn't hear God anymore because the light turned red and a freight train exploded across my quiet evening like an eight thousand ton package of screaming steel is inclined to do when you're sitting by yourself on the patio, outside a coffee shop, next to the train tracks.

14

A WALK IN THE PARK – PART 2

Marie crawled back into the driver's seat of the Jeep after locking the gates, securing our road into the restricted backcountry of Dinosaur Provincial Park. She had been working as a tour guide for almost three years and was having about as much fun as any paleontology major can have. As we drove further into the reserve, she detailed how she had been dividing her spring and summers between extracting dinosaur fossils, charting bone beds and escorting jeep loads of tourists like me on day trips to explore the mysteries in the park. I was happy there were only three of us in today's dig party: Marie, our guide; Beverly, a movie industry pro from Calgary; and myself. With such a small group, I was confident that I'd be able to stay involved in the ongoing commentary about fossils, erosion and all things dusty.

In several places the gravel roadbed was sliced clear through, washed out by the recent rains. The Jeep did its job effortlessly. I held on with one hand and listened as Marie explained how the Badlands had been formed. She pointed out sandstone formations, and hoodoos, and microfossil beds lining the roadway. After fifteen minutes of winding and lurching, she pulled our Jeep off the road and slid to a standstill with the hood pointing into the canyon. I stepped out into the Alberta sunshine, flung a Tilley hat onto my head and pulled my belongings out of the backseat. Marie marched around the hood of the Jeep and pointed out a tiny object sitting several hundred yards off our port bow, nestled on a shelf in a barren ravine. A smudge of weathered blue, almost invisible against a palette of earth tones. It was a picnic table. In such a vast landscape, washed out against the harsh rays of the morning light it was barely recognizable as a human artifact. We pulled some tool packs and a couple of plastic bins out of the cargo area, and began our descent into the canyon and out of sight of the avocado green four wheel drive, our only method of transport back to civilization.

For a boy raised on the coast where neighborhoods are routinely sliced in half by lush stands of towering Douglas firs, this stark landscape was made even less hospitable by the complete lack of trees. An all-encompassing palette of mottled sepia tones and sienna stretched as far as my wide eyes could see. Thirsty outcroppings of Russian thistle and foxtail barley, no more than waist high, clung to the sediment under our trail. Faded prairie grasses stood still for the moment, waiting for the inevitable midday winds to sweep into this valley. It was difficult to judge the size and nearness of the rocks and sandstone outcroppings that appeared before us. The blue September sky went on forever.

I altered my step, planting a hiking boot on a weathered piece of wood that lay almost entirely submerged across our pathway. A root perhaps, or lonely tree trunk brought down by a storm in years past. I looked around me in every direction to see if I'd overlooked any trees. "That big thing you just stepped on," said Marie, noticing my interest, "that is a piece of dinosaur bone, possibly a femur from one of the larger species. Every time it rains around here we get so much erosion that I never know what we're going to find once we get out into the field again." I turned and looked down at a smooth pale object about four feet long and nearly as wide as my boot.

"Don't worry about it," she said. "There are too many fossils out here to count, and we have so many adult specimens collected already. These days, our job is to retrieve all the evidence of adolescents we can find so we can learn more about their development and growth patterns."

In less than three minutes we arrived at that lonesome picnic table stationed a third of the way down the canyon wall. This would be our base camp for the day. I stared up and down a dry ravine and across the valley floor to a series of sandstone formations that appeared to be spilling out of the coulee wall in various places along a shelf similar to the one on which we were now standing. We were stationed perhaps halfway along a gulch that spilled into the Red Deer River Valley proper a few hundred yards off.

This small branch, one of dozens that cut through the sediment, was decorated with freshly formed rills, twisting channels carved into the sand deposits by the rain, a reminder that erosion was the only constant in these hills. Even the experts wouldn't venture a guess as to how many fossils had once lain in this sediment. Researchers could only choose from those left behind, exposed to the elements as the sedimentary layers were peeled away by wind and rain.

According to the official geology party line, the majority of this valley had been carved by the floodwaters of an ancient inland sea that lay three hundred kilometers to the east. Sixty-five million years ago, the Bear Paw Sea stretched from the Gulf of Mexico to the Arctic Ocean, dividing the North American continent in half. Marie explained that any dinosaur fossils we saw today would be the result of the seasonal flooding that had wiped out large herds of herbivore and carnivore alike.

"Not just ONE flood event?" I asked Marie, wondering if she would pick up on my biblical inference.

"Oh no, several different floods," she said without hesitation. "Sixty to seventy-five million years ago this locality would have flooded as easily as modern day Bangladesh. Herds numbering in the thousands were routinely caught in the hurricanes and wiped out. If their carcasses were covered by mud and earth before the scavengers could get at them, then fossils were able to form."

After I had unloaded a camera, lunches and tools onto the picnic table, I turned my attention to a weathered blue plastic tarp, about twenty by twenty, that lay a few paces behind us. The tarp covered a mound about waist high, and reminded me of a fresh cemetery plot. This was our dig site. What was under that tarp?

As Marie barked instructions, Beverly and I lifted sandbags and boulders from the perimeter of the tarp. I grabbed my corner as we carefully lifted it, and walked backwards exposing whatever lay beneath to the late September sun. I held my breath. Jumping up and down was out of the question. To make sure that both Marie and Beverly knew I was one cool paleontology hack, I dropped my corner of the tarp, turned away, and pointed my Nikon towards the distant edge of the canyon. Like it didn't matter that behind me lay several dozen dinosaur bones, entombed in a sandstone sarcophagus about fourteen feet across and almost four feet high. Like it was no big deal that in a couple of minutes I'd be crawling around in this ancient dust, running my fingers over the surface of fossils calculated to be 76.2 million years old—if you're okay with the math. Like I would ever let my fellow paleontologists know that on the inside I was a jumble of nerves, penitent as a monk on the steps of a storied cathedral and giddy as a snot-faced two-year-old in the ball room at McDonalds.

With all the cool standoffishness I could extract from my forty-something year old bones, I peered through the lens of my camera and zoomed in on a collection of man made objects, huddled together on the precipice of the far canyon wall about a half mile to the east. Tiny shapes dotted the skyline like plastic toy train buildings pushed to the edge of the kitchen table, mere silhouettes, insignificant against the expansive Alberta sky. With the slightest touch from a giant invisible finger, those buildings would teeter and then fall silently end-over-end, unraveling into tiny shards of wood and aluminum and concrete, scattered like yesterday's ashes across the Russian thistle and foxtail barley that adorned this ancient graveyard.

I put down my camera, adjusted my Tilley and turned to have a closer look at the most amazing sandbox I'd ever stepped in.

15
THE DEBATE

By the time the ninth grade in all its neurotic glory had swallowed me whole, I wasn't a child any longer. However, a lot of kids in my school, still holding to their childish ways, had decided that I was one of those people they'd rather not sit beside at lunch. This may have been because I sat marinating in my own gym strip, which hadn't seen a spin cycle since the Maytag Man had given up his blankie for Lent. Or maybe it was because I had not yet overcome my compulsion to suck up chocolate milk with a straw, hold it in one hand with my thumb over the top to maintain a vacuum, and then watch it swish back down through the straw, through the cafeteria air, thick with week-old grease, and back into the milk container. I was convinced that I sat alone during lunch because I was a Christian.

I had adapted to my loner lunch status quite well, and in part because I found myself in the same predicament during Algebra, Shop, English, History and Band. There were a few other Christians at my school, but they were such losers that I couldn't be seen with them. So to deaden the pain, ease my desperation and show the love of Jesus in a practical non-denominational way, I made the effort to hang out with Bradley Wagner, who was, in case anyone dared ask—an atheist. I had never known a real live atheist before. I'd read about one in a Billy Graham magazine I found on the coffee table when I was eleven. But he didn't stay atheist for very long. I guess that was the point of the story.

I had known Bradley Wagner since grade four. His family was moving into our subdivision one morning as I was walking to school. I had been distracted by the strange collection of artifacts emerging from the tail of a Hertz rental truck parked at 4380 Northland Drive, and I found myself watching for any signs of kids moving in. After witnessing the appearance of a floor-to-ceiling brass pole lamp, a harvest gold velvet Lazy-boy, and a dishwasher on wheels (where did the water go?) I caught a glimpse of something even better. From the shadows of the truck appeared a robin's egg blue laundry basket brimming with board games and jigsaw puzzles. The blue basket began its descent down the squeaky ramp hooked to the back of the truck. I didn't see a person, but the part I could see, a pair of squishy legs with dimpled knees stuffed into a new pair of blue suede Northstar running shoes, told me everything I needed to know. I focused on the contents of the laundry basket to get a quick read on the kid I surmised was behind it. Stock Ticker, Life, Operation, Trouble, Kerplunk, and a Ouija Board. Apart from the disturbing presence of some Parker Brothers branded occult paraphernalia, I now knew that everything was going to be okay.

Over the years, Bradley and I developed a great friendship and a unique style of communication. During the fourteen-minute walk home from high school, I could talk about almost anything, and he would just smirk or laugh out loud, but usually just smirk. Our conversation, which was actually more of a monologue because Bradley was a fan of single word volleys like "hhhyeah..." and "whatev...", touched on intense issues like unconditional love, the nature of God, how suffering could exist in a universe ruled by an omnipotent creator, and why fighting in hockey wasn't really a sin. For all my rambling, Bradley never cut me off. He didn't call me stupid names and he never once accused me of wrapping my brains in duct tape to keep the realities of the modern world from accosting my theological sensibilities.

That was Mr. Schelwaite's job.

Mr. Schelwaite taught physics, and I was in his class every year of high school, except in grade nine when I considered a switch in career paths and attempted chemistry. Apart from the time I used a Bunsen burner to light a fire in the hair on my forearms, I don't remember much about chemistry.

Mr. Schelwaite didn't believe in God, or in pants that went all the way down to where the socks hung out with the shoes. He had a neatly trimmed ring of flaming red hair that resembled a cul-de-sac on the top of his cranium, and a red beard to match. He was a mild, long-suffering man, with a ready smile, but when he'd had enough of your jacking around during one of his notoriously frantic overhead projector scribble-fests, his piercing eyes could burn into your soul like garlic in a freshly grated knuckle.

One day in tenth grade Mr. Schelwaite announced that we would be having a debate on the "ORIGINS OF LIFE." His haunting, deliberate delivery of "ORIGINS OF LIFE" reminded me of a bad vampire movie and was intended to evoke awe and drama. This was serious. The class would be given a week to prepare, and we were divided up into two teams. I ended up on the side defending creationism. Now by this point in my theological training, I had already learned about all those huge gaps in the fossil record, and I could draw most of the Old Testament characters on graph paper to show how their lives overlapped from Adam to Abraham, proving that God had created both the heavens and the earth around 4004 BC, give or take a few squares.

"A showdown between the Bible and Science… like taking candy from a baby chimpanzee," I whispered under my breath, and grinned. The class was dismissed to strategize, and suddenly my debating teammates surrounded me, like a pack of hyenas at a balloon crash site on the Serengeti.

"So where do we start?" asked one.

"Have you got any books on this stuff?" asked another.

"Will we win?" they inquired together.

"Can I finish your beef jerky?" asked Bradley.

He was not at all impressed with my newfound status as king of the non-apes. Or maybe he was irate at being asked to defend a theistic explanation of life when he didn't even believe in Theo. I was flustered, excited and embarrassed all at the same time. It was that same warm fuzzy feeling I got whenever a partial strand of DNA base pairs would drop off my body onto the linoleum and morph into Peruvian fruit bats. I never actually saw this happen, of course, but Mr. Schelwaite said that if we waited long enough, like a few giga-tri-billion decades, it was very likely to happen. Either in our universe or one of the other ones.

"Well," I started timidly, "Who here believes in God?" Nods all around. Followed by an emphatic "Duh!" from Bradley. The response was unanimous, and I was stunned. Every single student gathered around my lab table believed that somewhere—out there—was this personality that knew how the universe was put together, understood all the intricacies of bio-molecular diversity, had insider information that relativity wasn't just a theory, could sketch the periodic table on a napkin at lunch from memory, and even knew the expiry dates on every chocolate milk container in the bottom of my locker.

"Are all these people Christians?" I asked myself. "Well... no, they can't all be because Jenny Filger smokes, and she's wearing that tank top that fits way too tight again and, well, she just can't be! And Martin Palin has a mouth like Alfred Tong, who moved to bleepin' Saskatchewan after grade six. And Gerry Pendelson, well, Gerry doesn't believe anything for sure unless he reads it in *Mad Magazine*! And then there was Bradley. He didn't believe in God, so he'd be a huge liability as we got deeper into this. "Can we do trades?" I asked Mr. Schelwaite. No deal.

I was confused. I didn't know what to make of all my classmates acknowledging their believing in God, and not even having the common decency to look like church kids. Or act like church kids. And I wasn't at all sure how God was going to deal with the news, but I was positive he would not be happy with their lackluster Sunday school attendance records, and their smokes, or the Farrah Faucett posters plastered with bubble gum to the inside of their locker doors.

Looking back, I'm not sure that I had it all figured out at fourteen. Grace, I mean. And all the potential that God could see in people before I had a clue. But at this moment in time, higher notions were lost on me. Did it really matter that we were huddled in the back corner of Mr. Schelwaite's classroom hatching plans to deliberate on the creative intent of a God that cared even mildly about the ebb and flow of our young hormone-infested lives? No. All that mattered was that for this moment, for the first time since elementary school, when I burped my way to the podium on sports day, I was IT. THE man. A scrawny, nervous man without back hair, but THE man nevertheless.

I focused on the task at hand. We had a debate to win and it was my time to shine. As my adoring followers gathered wide-eyed around my lab table, I noticed Mr. Schelwaite sauntering over with a bounce in his step and a stupid grin on his face. Either he had just asked Simon Lawton to pull his finger, or he was coming to provoke us, to mock us. Us, with our silly notions of God creating the heavens and the earth, and Adam and Eve and Noah, and that freaking humungous ark big enough to hold every species on the planet—times two. I bit my lip and tried not to speak…or breathe. I stared at Mr. Schelwaite and then over his shoulder as Simon Lawton covered his nose, started waiving frantically and made a dash for the hallway.

§

Little did I know when we got slaughtered in the infamous Faith vs. Science Smackdown in room 324 that I wasn't the first Christian to have his spleen handed to him on a greasy cafeteria tray after a little disagreement over God's place in the scientific order.

I remember feeling outgunned and ill-prepared. Persecuted. Of course it would have helped if I'd known that in order to have a decent chance in any debate you must stick to the subject being argued about. Note to self: When one side argues that SCIENCE IS and the other side argues that GOD IS, that's not a debate. That is what they call in fruit grower's lingo— apples and oranges. The outcome at shindigs like these is always in the hands of whichever corporate sponsor has the biggest logo on the event poster. I was doomed from the start.

In time, I got over the embarrassment. I was too young to appreciate the hardship endured by generations of science geeks who had lived centuries before me and thrived, maintaining that God wasn't just another shiny object in some cosmic scavenger hunt, but that inquiry into the natural order was his intention for us all along. I was too young to know that this faith /science controversy had worn a dangerous path of its own out on the slippery slope.

16

A BRIEF HISTORY OF US AGAINST THEM — AM I MY BROTHER'S KEPLER?

"He set the earth on its foundations: it can never be moved."
~Psalm 104:5

Introspection is never easy. I avoid honest self-examination like I avoid eggplant sandwiches. But while an honest evaluation of my own bias is required from time to time, I had never summoned the courage to take my community of faith off its pedestal. What would I uncover if I scanned the surface for spider-vein cracks, hints of conceptual faults buried beneath the porcelain surface? Fortunately, I wasn't without a starting point.

Unfortunately, *The History of Western Civilization*, a rose colored 864-page textbook from my University days, lay somewhere on a dusty shelf at the Salvation Army thrift store, as ignored by bargain hunting book hounds today as it was by me until three days before my final exam over twenty years ago. I had come close to failing history once before, and now, compelled to repeat it, I headed for the nearest library with a simple plan. Dig, and dig some more.

I stepped timidly through the automatic doors of our community library, like I was sneaking onto the bridge of the USS Enterprise. I was certain that those who belonged here would recognize me in an instant as a fraud. I would be jettisoned back into the lobby where the ignorant masses ate Cheetos and scanned the bulletin board for cheap snowboards and bunk beds. But no one even noticed me as I gawked at the signage cantilevering off a concrete pillar in front of the library checkout. I almost blew my cover by asking a library assistant to point me to the card catalogue. Remembering that card catalogues had been banned the same year that home phones went cordless, I gathered my wits, scanned the overhead sign again and padded over to a cluster of computers.

After spending six uneasy minutes in front of the online catalogue, scribbling manically with a blunt-nosed golf pencil, and another twenty minutes flitting about the stacks like a thirteen-year-old in search of a decent song on the minivan stereo, I finally found what I was looking for.

After a forty-five minute tour of the stacks, I settled on thirty-six pounds of reading material that I was sure would re-awaken my interest in history and re-animate my waning biceps. What I hoped to discover was an outside perspective on how my Christian faith had fared against the advances of science. Perhaps hindsight isn't the fairest of lenses, but it is accurate. I scurried to the counter, checked out my books, and made a break for the safety of the library lobby. If I had any hope of scaling the ancient walls of the scientific establishment, I was going to need some energy. Now, where were those Cheetos?

Copernicus

Nicolaus Copernicus (1474–1543) was a Polish cleric who, like myself, spent much of his life within the confines of church life. Unlike me, he attended University in Krakow where he studied astronomy and mathematics, before venturing to Bologna where he focused on canon law. After his return to Poland, where he would serve as a cleric, Copernicus took up painting as a hobby. He also loved to translate poetry from Greek to Latin, but as the local Greek to Latin Poetry Club never did reach critical mass, he spent a lot of time alone.

His fascination with the heavens kept him painting during the day and taking notes under the dazzling midnight sky from a turret built into the wall of the Cathedral at Frauenburg. From that vantage point he theorized that the earth traveled around the sun once every year, all the while spinning on its axis once every twenty-four hours. While his understanding of theology was fluid enough to meld with this new discovery, church leaders ruled that biblical interpretation was the standard against which all observations in the physical realm would be measured. A major concern for the church authorities was that by displacing mankind, created in God's image, from his rightful position at the centre of the universe, and re-assigning him to one of many planets revolving around the sun, the faithful would no longer see themselves as superior to creation, and as special creations by God.

But the Copernican heliocentric model was not rejected outright by the church. The official position taken by Rome was that although it appeared as though the sun centered our solar system as measured with the naked eye, biblical authority, specifically Joshua's Old Testament account of the sun standing still, made that apparent fact an impossibility.

Martin Luther, who was preoccupied making his own observations regarding the centre of the ecclesiastical universe, and preparing to challenge the establishment on that front, agreed with church hierarchy on this matter. He found Copernicus' idea theologically impossible and morally bankrupt. He and his fellow reformers, including John Calvin, voiced their opposition to the absurd notion of a universe made up entirely of moving parts.

Copernicus didn't have the stomach for controversy, and grew tired of the name calling ("paint-sniffing heretic" was understandably hurtful) so he retreated to his hobbies of art, poetry and naked eye observations of the night sky, quite content to let someone else take the heat for his insights.

Shortly before his death in 1543, Copernicus' finally published his masterwork *Revolutionibus orbium coelestium* ("On the Revolutions of the Heavenly Spheres"). Too weak to argue with his critics, Copernicus could not prevent Andreas Osiander, a student of Luther from preparing an addendum to the preface informing the reader that heliocentrism was simply a theory, not a scientific fact. It would be decades before Johann Kepler would expose Osiander's ghostwriting shenanigans to the public.

(Even in the sixteenth century the word *theory* was proving to be a formidable foe to many Christian educators.)

Over the course of his lifetime, the Copernican idea had taken hold across much of Europe and wouldn't be dismantled easily.

From my vantage point in the twenty-first century, the notion that theologians would refute such obvious truths about nature seems silly. It was a simple misunderstanding, no doubt. As soon as some geek comes along with a decent telescope the argument will be settled, right?

Galileo

"I do not feel obliged to believe that the same God who has endowed us with sense, reason, and intellect has intended us to forgo their use." – Galileo[1]

Galileo furthered the Copernican ideas of planetary motion, but he did it with a telescope. Quite the entrepreneur at heart, Galileo published his *Dialogue Concerning the Two Chief World Systems* (1632) in Italian rather than Latin because he wanted to impact folks in the street, rather than church officials. Written as a series of fictitious debates between two philosophers and a layman, the book was a thinly veiled attempt to expose the flaws in the Ptolomaic system, which was approved by the church, and the Copernican position, which was not. Galileo even set up shop grinding lenses and manufacturing telescopes so that the public could actually see what he was proposing. Still, the clergy, who at that time controlled access to education, had him arrested and tried for heresy. Their Decree of 1616 stated clearly that Galileo's doctrines concerning the stability of the sun, and the motion of the earth, were contrary to the faith. Any cosmology that grouped all the planets into a different category than the stars might imply that those planets were like earth, complete with inhabitants, original sin and a Pandora's Box of theological implications.

For instance, would a second incarnation have been required at another time, on another planet? Would Jesus have to die again to redeem those civilizations? Would Leonardo da Vinci's famous painting have to be re-titled "The Second to Last Supper?" While the church authorities did consult with other scientific experts, opinions about Galileo's observations were divided. And the situation was complicated by lack of agreement as to

---

[1] Letter to Madame Christina of Lorraine, Grand Duchess of Tuscany (1615). In *Discoveries and Opinions of Galileo*, trans. Stillman Drake (New York: Anchor, 1957), 183.

whether the scientific community had the ability to lead on matters of natural observance without deferring to a literal reading of the Bible.

Galileo's frustration with church authorities hinged on what we today would call a misapplication of the scientific method. In short, the scientific method is a system for investigating phenomena in the material world and acquiring knowledge or correcting previously held facts based on the new observations. There is a lot of careful research to be done, hypotheses to be hypothesized, and experiments and facts to be checked. The following quote sums up Galileo's feelings:

> "On the other hand, if we were to fix only on what seemed to us the true and certain meaning of Scripture, and we were to go on to condemn such a proposition [as the motion of the earth and the stability of the sun] without examining the strength of the arguments, what a scandal would follow if sense experiences and reasons were to show the opposite? And who would have brought confusion to the Holy Church? Those who had suggested the greatest consideration of the arguments, or those who had disparaged them?"[2]

In the case of a heliocentric model of our solar system, the Psalms state emphatically that the earth's foundations don't move. Galileo's assertion was simply that from the perspective of the Psalmist, who was traveling around the sun at the same speed as the planet, and rotating on the surface of that planet at the same velocity as the sand under his feet, it could be said with full conviction that the earth's foundations didn't move. But to expand that notion to intergalactic proportions wasn't necessary, and therefore not in conflict with his (Galileo's) theory of planetary motion.

For his considerable efforts Galileo spent the last eight years of his life under house arrest, but was allowed to continue his discourse with the Church. Giordano Bruno, who preceeded Galileo by three decades, had also promoted a post-Aristotelian model of planetary motion. Bruno didn't receive the same generous treatment at the hands of his inquisitors. He was arrested after returning to Europe from a teaching stint at Oxford and had to endure a seven-year proceeding in Rome before being burned at the stake in the year 1600.

---

[2] Finocchiaro, Maurice A. *The Trial of Galileo: Essential Documents* (Indianapolis: Hackett Publishing Company, 2014), 90.

Kepler

Meanwhile, somewhere north of Tuscany, astronomer Johann Kepler (1571–1630) once again asserted that the earth was not the centre of our solar system, but that in fact our earth orbited the sun, in an elliptical orbit. He even had the audacity to reject perfect circles as having any place in his new astronomical model. This upset the church elders to no end, as every good Christian knew that God's favored geometrical shape was indeed the circle. (Centuries later, a bluegrass tune entitled "Will the Oblong Be Unbroken" would require a frantic rewrite to stave off yet another denominational splinter at the Grand Ole Opry).

To his credit, Kepler had more fight in him than his predecessors, and didn't let go of his cosmological theory, eventually proving through his brilliant mathematic equations with the help of some of the latest gadgetry that in fact the earth was not the centre of our solar system. Kepler's discovery of the laws of planetary motion were his way of "Thinking God's thoughts after him."

At this point in the faith/science conversation, people of the faith had found themselves painted into a curious corner. Was the Bible true or not? Had a Creator actually set planet earth on a foundation that was immovable, as stated so obviously in Psalm 104?

Were the assertions put forward by Copernicus, Galileo and Kepler simply misguided mathematical scribbling or diabolical heresy, capable of leading people into apostasy? What would become of the Christian faith in the face of an unbridled assault by these liberal quacks with their flawed gadgetry, a quick mind for numbers and predisposition towards the occult? And more importantly, how would believers carry on those purpose driven conversations with the heathen down at Starbucks? There was no question they would have all heard the commotion and were going to be making uncomfortable accusations about the Bible being outdated, and no longer relevant to the progressive sixteenth century mind! In fact, in one of his letters to his daughter, Maria Celeste, written during his house arrest, Galileo bemoaned the fact that truth seekers north of the Alps were converting to Protestantism because at least this new strain of Christianity had the courage to consider Kepler's discoveries as being consistent with biblical faith.

Newton

Within a few decades, Sir Isaac Newton began to make his mark as the founder of modern physics. He was also an astronomer, mathematician, theologian and the man single handedly responsible for turning calculus into a paying gig for thousands of eager calculus hobbyists. Newton also articulated the laws of motion, which laid the foundations for modern physics. In summary, they explain that:

1. Objects in motion stay in motion while objects at rest stay at rest (and are happier if they have an icy drink).

2. Force equals mass times acceleration.

3. For every action there is an equal and opposite reaction.

Sir Isaac also faced severe opposition by the Christian community for his other discovery—the universal law of gravitation. The good news was that this push back by the Church was undeniable proof of his aforementioned Third Law of Motion, which states that for every action there is an equal and opposite, and doctrinally motivated, reaction. Newton's gravitational law was seen as heretical because it proposed that unseen forces held the planets and moons in their respective orbits, and our entire solar system in its year long trek around the sun. This new cosmological assertion by Newton was never going to fly.

The purposeful inclusion of occult powers into the everyday operation of God's universe was frowned upon by Church leaders of the day. Gravity had to go. It appears that a pattern was being established that would only become more entrenched as men of science continued to explore, dig, dissect, exhume and theorize about the world around them. It seemed that those who invested their lives in the pursuit of God's laws found themselves on trial for breaking God's laws.

17

REWIND TO AUGUSTINE

While I was vaguely familiar with the accounts of Copernicus, Galileo, Kepler and Newton, I still couldn't figure out how after almost fifteen hundred years of relative peace between faith and science within the Christian conversation there had arisen such antagonism. Surely the Church fathers would have not been distracted by such off-purpose tangents? I found my answer when, one fortuitous Tuesday at the library, I bumped into St. Augustine.

You have to understand that as a lifetime member of the Evangelical community, I hold that all scripture is God-breathed, useful for teaching, rebuking, correcting and training in righteousness (2 Timothy 3:16). And that's just for starters. The infallibility of the Bible and the inerrancy of Scripture are foundational doctrines in my faith framework and have shaped my worldview since childhood. *Sola scriptura* as the early reformers used to spray-paint on the neighbor's barn, is Latin for "by Scripture alone."

This doesn't mean that all decision making regarding matters of faith must be found within the pages of Scripture. What it does mean is that all reasoning and investigation from the realms of my personal experience and deductive logic must bow under the authority of the Bible—as it is interpreted by either myself, my pastor, denominational board, small group leader, Sunday school teacher, college professor or parachurch ministry on any given Sunday. *Sola Scriptura* is a great slogan and would surely inspire awe if it were silkscreened on a t-shirt with respectable weave, the only real snag being that each person brings their own set of experiences to the table, and the resulting abridged version is actually more like *sola scriptura nisi vestri duco professor sententia*, which translates, "by scripture alone unless you're citing expert opinion."

Furthermore, as an evangelical, not only is a literal understanding of the Bible (where expedient) paramount to interpreting faith, but traditions held in common throughout much of Christendom are often frowned upon, if they are recognized at all. Until I had set foot in a Catholic Church with my in-laws several Christmases ago, I thought Advent was a method for tracking chocolate consumption. Sort of like keeping score with Weight Watchers except that the ultimate goal is a triglyceride count that exceeds your Facebook "likes." Church tradition has often been tucked away on the top shelf, out of the reach of curious little minds, in much the same way the Scripture was hidden from parishioners before the Reformation.

Well, you can understand my surprise the day I discovered the writings of Augustine, possibly the greatest Christian theologian after St. Paul. (To clarify, I did not personally discover the writings of St. Augustine. I simply unearthed them in the slacker's corner of my local library, resting under a copy of *Sports Illustrated*.)

Augustine was born in the fourth century, when the ink on the table of contents of our modern Bible was barely dry. His writings about scriptural interpretation were already causing nervousness for many within the faith community and for that reason alone I like him. A quote from his *The Literal Meaning of Genesis* is worth placing here in its entirety:

"Usually, even a non-Christian knows something about the earth, the heavens, and the other elements of this world, about the motion and orbit of the stars and even their size and relative positions, about the predictable eclipses of the sun and moon, the cycles of the years and the seasons, about the kinds of animals, shrubs, stones, and so forth, and this knowledge he holds to as being certain from reason and experience.

Now, it is a disgraceful and dangerous thing for an infidel to hear a Christian, presumably giving the meaning of Holy Scripture, talking nonsense on these topics; and we should take all means to prevent such an embarrassing situation, in which people show up vast ignorance in a Christian and laugh it to scorn. The shame is not so much that an ignorant individual is derided, but that people outside the household of faith think our sacred writers held such opinions, and, to the great loss of those for whose salvation we toil, the writers of our Scripture are criticized and rejected as unlearned men."

Augustine was just getting started:

"If they find a Christian mistaken in a field which they themselves know well and hear him maintaining his foolish opinions about our books, how are they going to believe those books in matters concerning the resurrection of the dead, the hope of eternal life, and the kingdom of heaven, when they think their pages are full of falsehoods and on facts which they themselves have learnt from experience and the light of reason?"

And just in case you were under the impression that the Church fathers didn't know how to throw down a proper insult check out this piece of hurt:

"Reckless and incompetent expounders of Holy Scripture bring untold trouble and sorrow on their wiser brethren when they are caught in one of their mischievous false opinions and are taken to task by those who are not bound by the authority of our sacred books. For then, to defend their utterly foolish and obviously untrue statements, they will try to call upon Holy Scripture for proof and even recite from memory many passages which they think support their position, although they understand neither what they say nor the things about which they make assertion."[1]

Even though Augustine penned these harsh words over fifteen centuries ago, I have concluded that the "reckless and incompetent expounders of Holy Scripture" he references should not be viewed as a

---

[1] St. Augustine, *The Literal Meaning of Genesis* (translated and annotated by John Hammond Taylor, S.J.) (New York: Newman Press, 1982), Vol. 1, 42-43.

metaphorical subset of the allegorical abstract. In this instance I hold to the literal understanding that he was one bottle of ink away from delivering a serious beat down on the entire Sunday school department. Augustine's angst (great name for a band by the way) was laser focused and prophetic. Was it possible that he could foresee the headaches that would become commonplace as the territory between what the scientific community could explain as true and what the Christian community could defend as true became more hotly contested? This chasm that separates our knowing from our believing, which was narrowing with each scientific discovery even in Augustine's era, has continued to close until presently, it's not much more than a teeny tiny gap. Unfortunately for many people of faith, this highly contentious sliver between the two tectonic plates of knowing and believing seems to be the only place left in our understanding where we can shoehorn in a compact and accommodating God.

18
GOD OF THE GAPS

There is a story in the Gospel of John about a woman, an alleged adulterer who was brought before Jesus. A posse of religious leaders had dragged her to the upstart preacher to see how he would respond. As is often the case in crimes of this type, the offending male was able to get away just in the nick of time. He may have jumped from a cathouse window to avoid the clutches of the Pharisees. (A tip for you guys over at CSI Jerusalem: LOOK FOR THE GUY WITH TWO BROKEN ANKLES AND NO PANTS!)

When the religious leaders suggested that he pass sentence on the woman, Jesus crouched down and started drawing in the sand. What did he write? Did he write at all, or was he just scribbling? Scripture doesn't tell us. I have heard differing opinions on what the mysterious sand writing may have included. Some say Jesus was writing the Ten Commandments as a set-up for his conversation with the crowd of accusers. Others say he was doodling. I wonder if he was drawing a line in the sand. We all draw our lines in the sand after all. It's our way of telling the difference between those who are on our side, and those who have, well, crossed the line.

In the case of science and faith, many on the faith side of the line have a well-documented history of being vocal about where that line exists. The problem, of course is that the line in the sand keeps moving. Jesus can draw lines in the sand whenever he wants. It's his sandbox. I, on the other hand, am beginning to wonder if it would be wise for me to opt out of the practice altogether.

The problem, as Augustine articulated, is that when Christians draw a line to explain where science ends and the work of God begins, science eventually comes up with some rather impressive evidence to explain how the work got done. And God is forced to retreat. This constantly moving divide between theology and natural processes has unfortunately dragged many skeptics along with it. I wonder if God, intent on letting his under-educated followers speak on his behalf, ever gets tired of this routine.

The phrase which best describes this line-sand-dragging argument is "God of the Gaps." This term reflects popular reasoning within the contemporary Christian worldview—"contemporary" meaning today, regardless of where today happens to sit on the grand timeline of history. When our understanding is limited, and it is always is, natural explanations for certain events are not always obvious. The person who says 'God did it' defers to the God of the Gaps.

In this framework, all the great mysteries of the age are secrets known only by God. Occasionally, he reaches into his vault of cosmic blueprints and drops another bolt of inspiration into the lap of a Kepler or an Einstein, but we must resist the urge to question things beyond our control. God keeps secrets from humans for good reason.

The difficulty with this position is that next week, when somebody comes up with a gadget to measure an event or an object—and explain it in physical terms—God has to retreat into the back room. Well, it's not God who has to step back, as he never stands in opposition to the truth. But God of the Gaps believers finds themselves in the uncomfortable position of having to admit that God wasn't the only way to explain an event. We are forced to sheepishly admit that through hard work, reason and even dumb luck, humans have discovered and refined the secret of fire, fermentation, crop rotation, electrical energy, the quarantine of viruses and stain resistant pants.

Thunder and lightning, for example, were beyond the scope of scientific measurement and explanation for thousands of years. So, whenever storms were accompanied by lightning strikes, and barns or cows burned to the ground, it was always God's fault. And who could blame him? There were so many things for him to be angry about. Insurance companies soon picked up on divine inclination to tantrums and "acts of God" were added to the list of ominous tragedies not covered by your monthly premiums.

However, as human technology advanced, an explanation for thunder and lightning and even the ability to forecast when and where it would happen next moved this act of divine moodiness into the realm of meteorology. We now know that lighting is the result of electrons in a cloud building up in contrast to a lack of electrons in another cloud or on the ground. The difference is referred to as electric potential or voltage, and when the built-up energy finally lets go, we see it as lightning, and experience the molecular rebalancing in the wake of the electric charge as thunder. And God, once considered the only logical answer to the question, is asked to relinquish all rights to the spectacle.

Other examples of God retreating to the fringes of our collective intelligence include germ theory, blood clotting and asteroids. God used to be responsible for all of that. Now he just watches on pay-per-view. As Jerry Coyne explains in his book *Why Evolution is True*, any creator that needs to jump in all the time to correct things is possibly less than the God we would want to worship.

It is important that "God of the Gaps" theory not be confused with a similar framework known as the "God has his reasons" thesis. In this scenario, God's laws aren't brought into question, merely his logic. When you're seven and you ask your mother why it hurts when you have a baby, she replies, "God has his reasons." What she really means to say is "Because he doesn't have to have them!" When you realize where a dung beetle gets its name, you say to yourself "God has his reasons." When you're at a potluck dinner and you come upon a Tupperware bowl brimming with bean salad, any person with a tongue and functioning cranial nerves asks the obvious question—why? Now God didn't make the bean salad; he can only take the hit for allowing the beans to survive the ice age, but the recipe is a result of free will. And God has his reasons.

19

THE FINE ART OF BEATING A DEAD HORSE (FLAT EARTH REVIVAL)

"That sun and moon and stars go round the earth
just as it seems,
and just as Scripture says they do,
and not as science dreams!"
— Excerpt from a poem, William Carpenter 1871

Now that I was finally up to speed with the middle ages and downright agitated with my foray into Augustinian literature, at least I could take solace in the fact that in the modernized world we had progressed beyond our superstitions and bronze age understanding of matter and the cosmos and all those crazy myths about a flat earth. Not so fast, says science historian Christine Garwood.

In her book *Flat Earth: The History of an Infamous Idea*, Garwood details a resurgence of Flat Earth theology that swept Great Britain beginning in

1830 and lasting well into the twentieth century. While I was intrigued, I wasn't sure if any of this flat earth stuff would help me sort through my origins puzzle. I would find out soon enough.

As the story goes, a flamboyant character with serious oratory chops and the stage name of Parallax was wowing audiences in town halls up and down the English countryside with his proofs of a flat earth. He had the science to support his thesis, or at least that's what many fundamentalists of the day believed.

Parallax, born Samuel Rowbotham, had been part of a religious commune up until 1830, when he became obsessed with defending the scientific truths of the Bible against the wild accusations of the advancing atheist hordes. He began preaching his flat earth position from the text of Psalm 104:5, which stated clearly that the earth has been set on its foundations and it can not be moved. Not satisfied with Galileo's insistence two centuries earlier that the darn thing was actually moving through the ether, Parallax resurrected fixed earth theory—geo-centrism. But he went one better. Rowbotham proposed that the earth was flat. (Contrary to modern belief, almost no educated person since the fourth century had any doubt that the earth was a globe.)

Rowbotham's traveling science/revival show proved quite entertaining to the Brits. With amazing persistence and showmanship, he garnered support from a sizeable chunk of the population. He also secured financial backing from some businessmen, including a small publisher and operator of a steam-powered printing press, who agreed to print and distribute Rowbotham's proofs of the true, non-globular nature of our planet.

The Flat Earth position, also known Zetetic Astronomy, can be explained as follows:

1. The earth is flat and round like a pancake. The North Pole is in the centre, and all the continents extend towards the outside edges, or circumference. Around the edge of this flat earth are first icebergs and then mountains of snow, to keep the oceans from draining out into space. There is no Antarctica. That's totally stupid. Unbiblical.

2. Mariners going 'around' the world are NOT really navigating a sphere. Their compasses always show true north (the centre), so they believe that they are traveling in a straight line, but they're actually moving either clockwise or counterclockwise. Just like a tetherball around its pole, but on a fixed plane. And by ship.

3. The sun doesn't actually rise or set. The planet is turning. We perceive the sun is setting (and perception is nine tenths of reality) because of refraction in our atmosphere. It's an optical illusion.

In the early 1800s, the natural sciences were only beginning to take hold as viable career options. Most of the science fraternity were ardent hobbyists, weekend warriors you could say, in the fight against geophysical ignorance. But they were no match for Parallax. His debating prowess was legendary, and whenever a debate did get beyond his grasp, he would simply vanish into the chilly English country air before his audience had clued in.

For almost forty years, Samuel Rowbotham frustrated the media and scientific establishment alike, and built a loyal following of trusting townsfolk with his nonsensical approach to Bible literalism and commitment to faith-fueled pseudoscience. The popularity of Flat Earth revival in the townships was accompanied by name calling in the press, with factions on both sides of the argument sounding off. Flat Earth evangelists would pay for full-page ads in the newspapers, warnings declaring the doom of England should the atheistic Newtonians gain a foothold with their anti-God theory of globe geology. (Is it just me or is this starting to sound familiar?) Some well intentioned but mistaken citizens even lobbied the government for a royal commission into the lies being perpetrated by the new breed of professional scientists that were growing in both number and status, and becoming a threat to the "traditional" Christian worldview.

Meanwhile, Thomas Henry Huxley, who had seized upon Darwin's recently published theory of Natural Selection and run with it zealously, was at the forefront of the new realm of Naturalism, which stated simply that empirical evidence found within nature, or the verified observations of physical things, was the surest method to declare whether or not something was true. While Naturalism was perceived by some as an attempt to remove God from the discussion of physical discovery, it was not an attempt to remove God from ALL discussion.

One of these naturalists was Alfred Russell Wallace, a contemporary of Charles Darwin. (Wallace is credited with pushing Darwin to publish *Origin of Species* under threat of being scooped.) Wallace made the decision to take the flat-earthers to task, and challenged them to a series of public experiments. The resulting war of words that played out in the papers was an embarrassment to those in the newly forming scientific elite. The Flat

Earth contingent were slick in their presentation, and debating prowess. Even with newly developed technology and supposedly impartial referees to keep the playing field level, the Flat Earth evangelists would not be an easy out.

Truth appeared to be hanging in the balance, with Wallace claiming on behalf of the secular establishment that the evidence was with them, while the Flat Earth contingent maintained that Scripture and ultimate truth was on their side.

Revival Comes to America

Across the Atlantic, an evangelist named Wilbur Glen Voliva had risen to national prominence, first as a faith healer and more notoriously as defender of Bible literalism. He had developed a serious interest in the intense Flat Earth debate going on in Britain and took up the cause. His church, the Christian Catholic Apostolic Church, based in Zion, Illinois, had over six thousand members and operated as a fully functioning town, complete with church-owned businesses and schools.

Voliva used his radio broadcast to preach against the two evils he felt were being foisted upon society by the scientific elite: round earth geology and Darwin's dangerous theory of evolution. He was such an accomplished orator that the prosecuting attorney for an upcoming trial scheduled to take place in Dayton, Tennessee added his name to a list of possible witnesses. William Jennings Bryan, the prosecutor in this small town trial that would take on national significance and circus-like proportions, had scribbled Voliva's name down, hoping the judge would accept his expertise in flat earth theory as part of a two-pronged attack against irreligion in taxpayer-funded classrooms. While Voliva was never asked to testify at the Scopes Monkey Trial, these two all-stars of Bible science came within a hairsbreadth, and one judge's pen, of appearing on the same stage in one of the most publicized trials in American history. It's hard to say how the subject of origins in America may have differed had the Scopes Trial been inexorably linked to those spellbinding flat-earthers.

Aimee Semple McPherson, the founder of the Foursquare Gospel Church (the denomination that I grew up in) centered in Los Angeles, had a rather public squabble with Voliva over his flat earth position, and was accused of trying to steal some of his congregation while he was preaching overseas. So while I have to admit to some hesitation in accepting my

Christian heritage in its entirety, I am very proud that Sister Aimee, as she was lovingly called during those revival days, was more than happy to stir the pot in this murky, quirky debate.

While the little town of Zion, Illinois prospered under the direction of Wilbur Voliva, he never lived to see his dream of flat earth theory reach into the public classrooms of America. He died in 1942 at seventy-two years of age, well short of the 120 years he claimed was promised by God as long as he fortified his diet with daily doses of Brazil nuts and buttermilk.

This might be a good time to wonder where the lunacy stops and the real science begins.

20
STANLEY MILLER

I n 1953, Stanley Miller became a rock star in labs all over the world when he successfully recreated the conditions thought to exist in the early stages of our universe. Ammonia, methane, water vapor (H_2O), and hydrogen were placed in a vacuum, and circulated by repeatedly boiling and condensing the mixture. As the gases flowed through the closed system, two electrodes protruding through the walls of a flask sent electrical sparks, like lightning, to interact with the gases.

After only a few days a red slime had begun to form on the walls of the flask. The slime was analyzed, and found to contain amino acids, the building blocks of proteins—the building blocks of life! By simply adding a spark of electricity to a jar of garden variety gaseous elements found lying about his apartment, Stanley Miller was able to produce eleven of twenty amino acids, apparently proving at long last that life on planet Earth was the result of nothing more than random chance. Since then, many have questioned whether the universe actually contained methane and ammonia as Miller theorized, but those early escapades spawned an entirely new field of exobiology, the study of biological matter outside the boundaries of our planet. Fifty years later, Stanley Miller is still celebrated.

I don't mean to belittle the importance of Miller's work in the field of abiogenesis, but I don't think that random chance accurately describes the process needed to get Stanley Miller's primordial soup cooking. Unless you consider following the lead of numerous cosmologists, chemists and planetary experts, meticulously assembling and orchestrating a system of select gases, sealed, thermally regulated and electrified with AC current supplied by the University of Chicago to be a random act with no creative intent, incontrovertible testimony to the tenacity of blind luck and jumper cables.

In his book *The Language of God*, Francis Collins (former head of the human genome project) argues that every scientist worth his weight in salt and hemoglobin dreams of making a discovery that will alter the playing field, just as Stanley Miller did in 1953. While Miller's conclusions have been revisited over the years, and his findings have been challenged, his celebrity status has never been in danger. Based on how the scientific community has treated Stanley Miller, Charles Darwin and others, it seems likely that dozens of budding biologists are looking to make a name for themselves by uncovering a brilliant twist on these original groundbreaking ideas.

And why simply tweak Miller's work on abiogenesis or Darwin's theory of natural selection? Why not overturn them entirely? In a culture where published papers can start a rookie on the long road to intellectual sainthood, and favorable peer reviews can guarantee tenure at the university of one's choosing, a Nobel prize and a tour on the late night talk show circuit, discovering a seriously respected new idea is the stuff science dreams are made of.

These serious new ideas live or die under the same rules that govern all of nature. Herbert Spencer, one of Darwin's biggest fans, coined the phrase that says it best: "The survival of the fittest." Ultimately, only those scientific theories that can withstand the scrutiny of other scientists will actually see the light of day. Peer review, as it is referred to in the industry, is the filter through which all new ideas must pass, more or less intact, in order to be considered real science. Scientific theories that are not robust— that don't fit with the evidence as determined by the community—get tossed aside like last week's celebrity diet books. And this is where all the commotion starts if you're a creationist.

To those of us who spend most of our lives outside the lab, this peer review process held in such high esteem by the elitists seems biased, corrupt and self-serving. At first glance, the dealer (the person in the white coat with letters all over their office wall) seems to be holding all the cards. And they get to deal those cards to whomever they want, or trust. How would a creationist go about getting his ideas heard by an unbiased jury of his peers—especially if he's the only Christian at the table? It appears that any attempt to include God as a variable in the equation will inevitably be shot down.

"You can't bring God into the lab!" says the evolutionist.

"Bring us evidence. We want hard facts, research and statistics. Give us something with which to do our due diligence," says the non-theist gleefully.

"But I do have evidence," replies the creationist. "It just so happens that God is sort of, well, he's tied up in the whole scenario. I mean look at the trunk on that elephant. You think that just happened? Look over there. It's an eyeball. You think that just happened?" It is near this point in the conversation that tempers are hot enough to melt hockey pucks.

Creationists love to attack evolution, convinced that Darwin's theory has been propped up by the scientific community simply because it appears to do away with God. "There isn't any real evidence for evolution," we've been told over and over and over. "They won't accept the notion of an all powerful God, so believing themselves to be wise they have become fools." Often Scripture verses are interjected to make it clear that this is not merely the opinion of fallible men, but of God. I am very familiar with the tone of these conversations because I've started them. However, what I am starting to recognize is that the restrictions built into the scientific method, specifically a predisposition against faith, which I always found unfair, are, as it turns out, the only way to make sure that science gets it right.

Geology, for example, by its own rules, can't arbitrarily decide the earth is only six thousand years old because it wants to. The geology department at my local university can't base the age of the earth on an antiquated Hebrew document just because. A young earth hypothesis must be backed up with facts. An ancient earth hypothesis must be backed up with facts.

Whichever hypothesis is able to make the most logical sense of available evidence becomes the favored theory. Every so often, in every field of research, a new piece of evidence turns the whole conversation on its end and the parameters of the debate are reframed. This is how science works. And this is to be expected when our knowledge is provisional, limited to those objects or ideas which can be touched, tasted, measured, weighed, melted, mixed and organized into familiar patterns.

As a Christian, if I maintain that these limitations support naturalistic explanations at the expense of theological ones, I would be only half right. The trade-off built into the equation is that a scientific theory playing by its own rules does not have the authority to wade into theological water. Discussions of God don't hang on things we can touch, taste, measure, melt, mix or store in a shoebox. So while an evolutionary biologist can refuse to accept my God hypothesis, he or she cannot, based on any scientific evidence, and in clear conscience, rule for or against the existence of God. While both theism and atheism can be considered statements of personal belief (or non-belief, in the case of the atheist), science is just science, which really takes all the pressure off when you think about it.

Back in the 1960s, at the height of the Cold War, while North Americans curled up in their lazy-boy rockers wondered how long we would live if somebody in the White House ever picked up that red phone and ordered a nuclear holocaust TO GO, starving Russians waiting in line for cheap gas and potatoes wondered the same thing. Yet in laboratories on both sides of the Atlantic, communist and capitalist researchers racing to solve the secrets of everything from neutron bombs to Tang all came to the same conclusion—if the neutron bombs don't kill us all, Tang will.

It turned out that believing or disbelieving in God didn't alter what calculus and the periodic table had to say about the escape velocity required for a successful satellite launch. Scientific illumination wasn't beholden to a team of Presbyterian rocketeers from Princeton any more than it was to those godless Commies from the Great Bear.

21
MATE

I know a guy named Charlie. We used to work in the same office before he got hired as a pastor and left the work force. What I mean is, he left the ranks of the merely employed and joined the ranks of the truly called. Much better.

In the workspace we shared for over four years (our desks were separated by an abandoned cubicle) it was easy for me to overhear his sales calls, which was okay with me because his phone manners were impeccable. Whenever he was faced with a client that needed to be educated about our company products, he was patient and thorough.

The only down side of sitting near Charlie was that I had to put up with his love of a South American beverage called mate (pronounced mah-tey). Four mornings out of five, the gentle, soothing aroma of my morning mocha would be obliterated by the noxious yerba fumes that billowed from a slender silver mug stationed twelve feet away on Charlie's desk. One morning, I became particularly distracted by the aggressiveness of the mate molecules as they escaped Charlie's cubicle. I put down my pen, reached for my mild mannered java and headed to where I knew I'd find Charlie sitting back in his office chair sipping intently on a gnarled silver straw.

I had spent the past few nights digging around for insight on the Genesis flood and needed a way to process this knowledge with a friendly voice. I had never realized, for example, that the capacity of Noah's ark had been no problem for Bible literalists in the Middle Ages. But it turns out when you add a few thousand new species from each of the newly discovered Americas and Australia to Noah's guest list, the challenge of fitting even more animals and food on board an ark of fixed size becomes ludicrous. And the eventual discovery of hundreds more dinosaur species, starting in the 1800s, did nothing to ease the squeeze on sleeping arrangements or boost the credibility of a the biblical flood story that, according to young earth creationists, was global in scope and involved the migration of species from every continent to the launch point.

As Charlie and I chatted about the morning traffic and the joys of car shopping, I let it slip that I was dabbling with some alternate interpretations of the book of Genesis. I figured that my willingness to discuss flood geology and how certain eighteenth century interpretations of Genesis were in desperate need of a makeover would make for great water cooler chat. I guessed wrong. Charlie wasn't as casual about this Genesis business as I'd hoped, and I could tell by the sudden reddening in his face that I had sauntered totally unprepared in hostile territory.

I should also mention that Charlie has a British accent, which can make his opinion on almost every subject sound more authoritative than it would otherwise. As he becomes more animated he can come off as slightly loony—in a loveable BBC British comedy sort of way.

"What are you talking about?" said Charlie with conviction.

"All I'm saying, Charlie, is that Noah's flood didn't necessarily have to cover the entire face of the planet."

"What?!" Charlie leaned forward in his desk chair and began gnawing on his mate straw. I glanced down at his tribal breakfast ritual of warm, wet, sub-equatorial sawdust.

"According to a Bible scholar that I've been reading, the Hebrew word that we translate as "earth"—*eretz*—is more often translated as ground or land as in '… and the water covered the whole *land.*' If that's the case, then the image of a universal flood, a world-wide deluge that so many Christians have in their minds when they think of Noah may not be quite… accurate."

"Well, that's all well and good to suggest that Genesis doesn't really mean what you thought it meant," said Charlie, "but Jesus, who happens to have a rather serious claim on the authorship of the entire Bible, referred to 'The days of Noah.' Are you saying that Jesus didn't know what he was talking about in the Gospels? Or that he didn't know what *eretz* actually meant? Is that what you're saying?"

I took a small step backwards. Charlie wasn't standing yet, but I didn't want the tension to escalate, or get caught flat-footed if he had an evangelical lunge coiled up inside him. I imagined the slow and painful rehab I would have to endure if Charlie lost control of his faculties with a scalding mate in his fist. I took another step back.

"Well, uh... I wasn't exactly suggesting..."

"What exactly were you suggesting?"

"Calm down. I am reading a book. This guy might be an idiot for all I know. I mean, look around you. Practically anybody can write a book these days."

Silence.

Charlie looked me square in the eyes and drew a slow, deliberate breath. "Don't go there!" he said firmly. "Once you've started down that path, there is no end in sight!" His British accent, now cranked all the way up to stun, was almost paralyzing. Poetic. Shakespearean in its beauty. I stood for a moment contemplating the error of my ways. What had ever possessed me to consider such exegetical lunacy? And to dare speak of it in the casual nonchalance of West Coast Canadian English?

The phone on Charlie's desk lit up. Mercifully, he turned away and took the call. I shriveled back into my corner, past the empty cubicle—a sadly lacking DMZ in this tiny, dangerous office. I spent the remainder of the afternoon at my desk, a defeated, wannabe progressive Old Testament scholar, likely *the* worst Old Testament scholar in the entire *Eretz*.

22
NOAH

The great flood, one of the most well known stories in the Bible, has captured the imagination of historians, archaeologists, and geologists alike. From the birth of the earth sciences, while some have attempted to rule the scriptural account fanciful and a total fabrication, others are convinced that somewhere, either in or under the ice and glacial till deposits of Mt. Ararat, lies buried the wreckage of the most famous watercraft in the whole of ancient zoological mariner history: Noah's ark.

While I am a huge fan of the ark, and would be tempted to hop the red eye to Istanbul the moment any substantive news were to come out, some days I wish that Noah had dropped anchor on this side of the Atlantic, where tourism and marketing would have room to work their magic.

Imagine the hype, for example, if Noah and crew had run aground in the Gulf of Mexico near present day Pensacola. Who would get the marketing rights? While SeaWorld seems like the obvious first choice, I think Universal Flood Studios also has a nice ring to it. Odds are, Disney would outbid them both. But for slack winds and an absolute dearth of navigational prowess Noah would now be doing daily photo sessions with Buzz Lightyear at the foot of Splash Mountain where, at precisely 9:15

every evening, a life size reconstruction of the ark would rise from the waters of Liberty Square escorted by a bevy of holographic mermaids performing a synchronized swim routine with a pair of hippos decked out in sailor suits. And we'd cheer wildly and shell out another six bucks for a churro to keep that Disney glow on the faces of our children as they basked under the shock and awe of *The Happiest Place on Dry Ground.* On the way to the parking lot we'd wander down Main Street Mesopotamia past gift shops laden with t-shirts with sayings like "Ark, who goes there?" or "Ark the 'Erald Angels Ing" or "I went to the Diluvial Kingdom and all I got was this dumb shirt."

As wonderful as that all sounds to those of us praying for more biblical relics to take their rightful place among the commercialized and exploited, Noah's ark didn't come to rest in Florida. It stayed pretty close to home until the water level dropped and it came to rest on the side of an indistinct mountain somewhere in the Turkish out-lands.

The Turks, as it turns out, promote their national historic sites very differently than we do here in North America. They don't. The whole Ararat region has been practically cordoned off with yellow police tape for the better part of a century. Due to more than a century of seasonal skirmishes between the Turks and the Kurds, Ararat is not always open for business these days and definitely doesn't extend park hours during Spring Break.

The reason I bring up Noah's ark at all is because creationists maintain that the Genesis flood was global—that God in his judgment of mankind flooded the entire planet—Mexico, Australia, the Alps, Topeka. Not only did every man, woman and child not aboard the ark meet their end, but every gazelle and koala bear except for two also drowned in an angry vortex of water, mud and divine wrath.

Any theory of a young earth demands that all of the geologic upheaval and fossil history we see around us be explained in relation to events within the last six thousand years. So while I hadn't intended to get sidetracked with Noah's story, I couldn't see any way to avoid a slight diversion into flood geology.

§

In 1923, against the tide of prevailing scientific thought, a school teacher from New Brunswick named George Macready Price published his seven-hundred-page masterpiece *The New Geology*. Fortunately for the environment, it wasn't a runaway bestseller.

Macready Price was following the lead of Ellen Gould White, the Seventh Day Adventist prophetess who had published her visions of a worldwide cataclysm. Macready Price argued that the geological formations on every continent are a direct result of the Genesis deluge. He theorized that a planet-jarring event, possibly an asteroid, had tilted the earth on its axis 23.5 degrees, causing the first tides and the accompanying mayhem. As an opponent of Darwin's theory of natural selection on the grounds that it seemed to reduce man to a mere beast, Macready Price focused his energies on geologic matters and ushered in the age of the Bible scientists.

If we follow the premise of a worldwide flood, an investigation of the geologic record should turn up plenty of evidence to support this interpretation of the story. However, a century and a half before Macready Price published his book, many other "natural philosophers" of the late eighteenth century had already been busy out in the field, launching geology as a legitimate field of study. Leading the charge into the mountains and gravel pits all over the countryside to bring clarity to the flood issue was an adventurous gang of pastors and Bible teachers. These mountain men, these heroes with shovels seemed to have it right. In their initial excitement they intended to prove beyond any doubt that Scripture could be counted on as a reliable source of knowledge concerning natural history. However, as evidence began to accumulate, many seekers began to question the commonly held assumptions about a universal flood.

Adam Sedgewick (1785–1873), for example, a geologist, teacher to Charles Darwin, and an evangelical Christian, publicly recanted his diluvial (global flood) position upon retiring the presidency of the Geological Society of London in 1831.

> "There is, I think, one great negative conclusion now incontestably established -- that the vast masses of diluvial gravel, scattered almost over the surface of the earth, do not belong to one violent and transitory period. It was indeed a most unwarranted conclusion… We saw the clearest traces of diluvial action, and we had, in our sacred histories, the record of a general deluge. On this double

testimony it was, that we gave a unity to a vast succession of phenomena, not one of which we perfectly comprehended…"[1]

What Sedgewick was getting at in his farewell speech to the Geological Society was that the geological theories of the time, which assumed a global flood based on common scriptural interpretation, had to be approached with fresh eyes.

A contemporary of Sedgewick, Charles Lyell, had recently published his three-volume masterwork *Principles of Geology* in 1830.

Principles set down the laws of uniformitarianism—the idea that gradual change over extremely long periods of time presented a more accurate model for understanding geologic formations. Lyell even suggested (very politely to those trying to muscle a violent cataclysm into the Genesis flood story) that the appearance of a "fresh" olive branch in the mouth of the dove sent out by Noah, was an indication that the rising and receding of the waters had been a comparatively gentle process which hadn't swept away topsoil or vegetation. Lyell's argument against a global deluge included evidence suggesting that elevated lakes such as the Black Sea, and ancient seismic events could have triggered a horrific *local* flood very similar to what was recorded in the Book of Genesis. However, the Hebrews weren't the only ancient tribe with such a story.

Other ancient cultures held their own variations on the flood theme. One of these, the *Epic of Gilgamesh*, is centuries older than the Mosaic writings and is the most significant work in all of Mesopotamian literature. *Gilgamesh* was translated painstakingly into English from a series of cuneiform tablets unearthed in the Royal Library at Ninevah, and dated back to the Assyrian Empire. It chronicles the life of the legendary King of Urak (Iraq) who embarks on a search for the meaning of life and travels to find Upnapishtim, an old sage who survived the great deluge by building a boat big enough to hold him, his family and all the animals. In another account, at the other end of the continent, *The Rigveda*, an ancient Hindu legend, tells of a solitary flood survivor named Manu who was warned by a fish that a flood would engulf all the creatures. He was instructed to build a ship so he could escape to the northern mountains. The Chaldeans (a polytheistic culture, ancestral family of Abraham) had their own flood story,

---

[1] Clark, John Willis, Thomas McKenny Hughes, and Adam Sedgwick, *The Life and Letters of the Reverend Adam Sedgwick* (Cambridge: University Press, 1890), 370.

which told of a ship coming to rest on the mountains of Nazir, before a dove was sent out to find dry land. Their story ended with a sacrifice and a feast. One jubilant goddess celebrated the end of the flood by tossing her bedazzled necklace into the heavens as a sign that the world would never again be flooded.

With all these ancient flood narratives floating around, including the Hebrew version in Genesis, it is no surprise that a team of scientific types would eventually get caught up in speculation.

Walter Pitman and William Ryan, American geophysicists, found themselves in the spotlight after a round of stellar underwater research in the 1970s. In their book *Noah's Flood: The New Scientific Discoveries about the Event that Changed History*, they detail how a research project originally focused on climate change, aboard a core-sample drilling rig in the Mediterranean, became a springboard in their search for evidence of Noah's flood. Their data showed that the Mediterranean basin had at one time been a semi arid desert, dotted with freshwater pools and isolated from the Atlantic Ocean. About 90,000 years ago, the Atlantic burst through at Gibraltar, converting the great plain back into a body of salt water, the Great Sea. Pitman and Ryan couldn't help but pose the question: Could the conditions that existed at that time, before human settlement and language developed, have occurred more recently, in a location closer to the cradle of civilization?

They were convinced the ancient flood stories were all based on a true historical event and that there must be evidence for it somewhere. After the Cold War ended and they were able to share their findings with fellow researchers from the former Soviet bloc, as well as Turkey, they laid out a compelling case known as the Pitman Ryan Hypothesis.

Relying on evidence showing how the Mediterranean basin had morphed from salt water to fresh water, to arid plain and back to saltwater sea again, they performed a similar series of core drilling exercises and sonar readings in the Bosphorus Strait and northward into the Black Sea. Their geophysical research, combined with independent archaeological findings and agricultural analysis, showed conclusively that around 5600 BC, the Aegean Sea had burst through a natural earthen dam near present day Istanbul.

Millions upon millions of gallons of salt water, powered by the hydraulic force of the world's oceans, cascaded into the landlocked and mostly arid Black Sea basin. While recent studies have questioned the variance in elevation between the two bodies of water, most experts agree the spectacle would have dwarfed any show we can witness today at Niagara Falls. The data indicates that the water bursting forth "from the deep" continued its assault on the landscape for over three hundred days.

As the salt water poured in, it combined with the fresh water in the lake, creating a toxic marine environment, and everything living in the Black Sea died. The fertile perimeter of the lake, home to tens of thousands of Neolithic farmers enjoying their first taste of agricultural success, became submerged as the lake rose six inches a day, killing anything or anyone incapable of staying ahead of the surge. Those who escaped with their lives were scattered in every direction and lived out their lives in Europe, China, Egypt and Mesopotamia. And they took their story of that terrible flood with them.

In 1999, following the lead of Pitman and Ryan, Bob Ballard, famous for his underwater discovery of the Titanic, began scouring the floor of the Black Sea. He was successful in finding human settlements three hundred feet below the surface and about twenty miles from shore, exactly where Pitman and Ryan predicted the ancient shoreline ended and human settlement began. Ballard's team also extracted mollusks from the sedimentary layers under the lakebed and found further support for Pitman and Ryan's theory. Seven species of saltwater shells were dated at 6,800 years or younger. Two additional species of extinct creatures, located deeper in the core samples, were dated at between 7,500 years and 15,000 years old. The Black Sea had in fact turned from fresh water to salt water in a recent cataclysm.[2]

Even today, as the buoyant fresh water of the mysterious Black Sea flows south gently into the Aegean and onwards to the Mediterranean, an underwater canyon hidden in the depths of the Bosphorus strait directs a torrent of salt water from the Mediterranean over a precipice and down a 450 foot solid granite flume—upstream into the Black Sea, just as it has been doing for the past 7,500 years.

Take that Splash Mountain!

---

[2] Ryan, William and Walter Pitman, *Noah's Flood: The New Scientific Discoveries About the Event that Changed History* (New York: Simon & Schuster, 1998), 146.

23

SUB SANDWICH

My musician friend Dan lives in a house perched on a heavily sloping lot under the canopy of the soggy North Shore Mountains of Vancouver. The sixty-five foot descent from my car to Dan's back door was its own small adventure, and I wouldn't have made it if I hadn't been able to feel my way along the soggy biomass on my butt. After maneuvering around a few Douglas firs and a healthy crop of spiny wood ferns embedded in Dan's privately owned slippery slope, I landed on a cedar deck that hung off the back of a cozy West Coast split-level. This piece of property was a metaphor for Dan's place in the cosmos. Not satisfied with hiking his way through every watershed plain in the Canadian North, Dan had gone out and purchased his very own rainforest. Sort of a *Jurassic Park* meets *Gorillas in the Mist*. Minus the gorillas. Add one propane barbeque and a rusty hose reel.

"You won't be able to convince anyone," he said with resignation in his voice, as we stood around the island in his kitchen stirring our coffees. I told him I was attempting to pull the biblical Noah story apart and make some sense of it. I wanted him to help me.

"Why not?" I asked. "You're the geologist. You are the guy who started me on this freaky ride! I remember your exact words: '… I've been a geologist my whole life and there is no way the earth is only ten thousand or ten million years old.' Oh, and thanks for jumpstarting my career as a heretic."

"You're welcome. Not everyone is willing to mess with their fondest held beliefs just for kicks. Like you're doing now."

"Just explain the geologic column to me."

"What do you want to know?" he asked.

"Is it real? The creationists are telling everyone that it doesn't even exist. That it's a half-baked idea to help sell the supposed age of ancient rock formations. You know, hundreds of millions of years worth of earth history jammed onto one whiteboard. The Bible science guys maintain the logic is flawed."

"Bible science? That's what they're calling it now?"

"No. That's what I'm calling it."

"The logic isn't flawed," said Dan. "And it is true that the geologic column doesn't exist in its entirety in any one place on the planet. But neither does the periodic table of elements unless you're counting lab posters and t-shirts. But that doesn't mean that we can't piece together sections from around the globe to assemble a complete picture of geologic history. By identifying plant and fossil material in each layer, we know which layers are older because we can follow the progression from simpler organisms to the more complex ones."

"And that's why creationists don't like it," I said. "Because you've already pinned your tail on the evolutionary donkey, so to speak. Creationists don't agree that the simpler organisms are necessarily older. They accuse the evolutionists of using circular reasoning. If it's already been decided that the simplest life-forms are older, then the rock formations containing those fossils are also the oldest. That's a problem, isn't it?"

"Only if you've pinned your own tail on a ten-thousand-year-old planet. If you hold to a literal interpretation of Genesis, a literal interpretation of an English translation of a 2,500 year old Hebrew transcript, than yeah, there is a problem. However, if you are just looking at the physical evidence, and that's what real science does, then the fossil record is an accurate timepiece and it tells us a lot."

"Because the older fossils like the dinosaurs are lying under the more recent fossils—the vertebrates and mammals?" I queried.

110

"Yeah, that's pretty much it," he said. "The theory behind the geologic time scale is pretty straightforward; any formation of rock is considered older than the rock that lies above it, and younger than the rock that lies below it.

"I've got an idea," I said. "What if I go buy a foot-long sub sandwich and come back to your house, and we put on goggles and get out your drill and one of those bits that takes tiny core samples and… It might get messy, but you'd be able to explain to me how the layers in the geologic column resemble the layers in a sub sandwich."

"And we are doing this WHY?" he asked.

"I need a visual, something to really drive it home."

Dan looked at me like this wasn't my best idea ever.

"This would be awesome," I said. "I can be back here in fifteen minutes. We'll duct tape a twelve-inch Italian Oregano Meat Lover's Special to your kitchen table and we drill down into it…not your table, just the sub." I paused to let the brilliance of my idea sink in.

"And what should happen," I continued, "is that we always find the lettuce lying on top of the tomato, and the tomato will always be on top of the cheese… and it shouldn't matter where I decide to drill. All the layers should always be in the same sequence from top to bottom because the order in which they were originally laid down is consistent. Did I get it right? Will this make for a good illustration?"

"Uh, yeah. Especially if we take a chop saw and slice the sub into three smaller pieces and force the middle section to ride up over another piece, like tiny Italian Oregano tectonic plates. Now if you drill at that location, you'll see tomatoes way higher in elevation than where we normally find tomatoes. Sort of like when they discover marine fossils in the Himalayas. It's not a sign of a universal flood. It's a sign that a chunk of the earth's crust has been forced upwards.

I sensed Dan was warming to my idea as he continued. "Oh, and you might not always find any tomato between the lettuce and the cheese."

"Because tomato slices have holes in them?" I wasn't sure.

"Because," said Dan, "because all the layers don't exist everywhere. This is where the creationists get it right. You might drill at one location and not find cheese or mustard. But wherever you drill you'll be able to make note of which layers are positioned next to other layers… and eventually you'll have a complete picture of the entire sub sandwich from top to bottom. Even when we drill at different locations on the sandwich, we'll get an accurate piece of the story."

"Oh, you mean that if we find a partial sequence of sandwich layers, say mayo on the top, and then lettuce and tomato, and then down through the cheese and ham in one location, and then at another drill site we don't find any lettuce or tomato, but we discover cheese on top of ham, and then discover turkey and mustard, we should be able to assemble an entire sequence, the complete sandwich making history, starting with mayo on the top, lettuce, tomato, cheese, ham, turkey and finally mustard on the bottom."

"Yup. You would have assembled an accurate history of the entire sandwich by taking snapshots at two different locations," said Dan.

"Unless the creator of the sandwich was trying to trick us by moving the mustard from below the ham to above the turkey at the other end of the sub, to mess with our infantile sense of reasoning?"

"Look… I have a career," said Dan. "We are not going to do this."

"Too messy?" I asked.

"Waste of a good sandwich," said Dan.

24

THOMAS: A MISUNDERSTOOD SKEPTIC

"Follow the argument wherever it leads" ~Socrates

This is the mantra repeated daily, like the Pledge of Allegiance, in science labs all over the world. Worn like a badge of honor by every proud member of the scientific fraternity. The history of science attests to it. From Plato, who said it first, or at least secured the copyright, to Socrates, and down to Galileo to Newton to Einstein and Hawking. Every time somebody unveils a new and improved model that illustrates how the natural world works, the old model gets set aside. It's the way we learn.

It is a curious thing that men and women, driven by their desire to assimilate facts and make sense of the world, too often find themselves objects of scorn. Like a gifted athlete heckled mercilessly by under-qualified and over-imbibed spectators, incapable of stepping out of the bleachers to offer any real help, the rational elite among us pay a heavy price for daring to ask questions.

While I doubt God sits on the stairs at MIT waiting nervously for the latest lab results, I don't think he expects that we do anything less. He created a universe that acts very predictably. So predictably, in fact, that we call those actions we can follow with any degree of certainty, laws. Sometimes it takes a few thousand years before humans are able to make sense of these laws. But every time we do, we uncover a little more of the wonder of creation. Trouble is, we don't all arrive at the same conclusion at the same time and, as history shows, it can be a dangerous thing to arrive at the right answer a couple of hours behind schedule.

Case in point: one of the first followers of Jesus Christ. Of the twelve disciples, the most maligned person in the New Testament not named Judas, is Thomas. Doubting Thomas (as he is now known by his millions of critics) made the mistake of not believing the other disciples when they tried to tell him that Jesus had come back to life after his execution at the hands of the Roman torture machine. We aren't told whether he actually wanted to believe or not. If he was like most first century Jews, any conversation of an actual resurrection—a human body beginning to function after it had been decaying for three days—would have been a non-starter. In John's Gospel, Thomas is quoted as saying that unless he could see the nail prints in Jesus's hands, and trace the wound in Jesus's side with his own fingers, he wouldn't believe their tale. Thomas's skepticism, based on everything he knew about the way that nature operated and the laws that it followed, compelled him to speak up. He challenged the other disciples to provide some evidence to back up their claim. Thomas is often portrayed as having no faith, of being too cynical. But all he ever asked for was some proof. Well, not just some. He demanded they produce a body, and that it be living, and that it be Jesus.

It is easy to sit here almost two thousand years after the event and accuse Thomas of being skeptical. Faithless. But all he really wanted at that moment was something, anything in the physical realm for his brain to mull over before his faith could be activated. To be fair, Thomas didn't have any less faith than the other disciples. (Read that last sentence again.) The other disciples had been present the first time Jesus appeared in the upper room, so they were in no position to accuse Thomas of lacking anything except timing. We could speculate on why Thomas was nowhere to be found when Jesus showed up the first time. Maybe he was out sleuthing at the sketchy end of town trying to figure out who stole the body. Maybe he was the only one with the guts to leave the upper room and go check the mail.

Whatever the reason, Thomas was missing in action when a brand new conversation broke out. He was totally unaware of the new reality and the flood of new data that turned the entire story on its head. Like the kid on your museum field trip that let go of the rope and spent the whole afternoon in the gift shop instead of the whale exhibit. Kid doesn't realize that the rest of the class learned all about plankton and blow-holes while he wandered around staring at key chains and Orca Pezz dispensers. Maybe "Distracted Thomas" or "Curious Thomas" would have been a more accurate nickname to duct tape to this poor guy's backside for the duration of Christendom. Fortunately for Thomas, the answers he didn't find on the street were answered in dramatic fashion when Jesus showed up in person for a second time.

So back to the logical, enquiring souls who spend their lives piecing together the mysterious fabric of our natural world. Are they doubters or just inquisitive? Are they scouring the evidence looking for clues, working with natural laws and well-tested equations out of a sincere thirst for knowledge or are they driven by less noble intentions? While none of their reasoning faculties are in opposition to God, too often the community of faith has mistaken their predisposition to the scientific method as a direct assault on our faith and our God.

I'm not convinced, as I once was, that science doesn't want anything to do with God. Instead, I'm starting to see that science isn't qualified on its own admission to offer any opinion on whether or not he is. This is very good news.

25

PORT TOWNSEND

I t was half past five on a chilly March morning, and I couldn't sleep. It may have been because of the incessant roaring of the tide beyond the sliding doors of our motel room in Port Townsend, Washington. For the record, evaluating why you are awake in the middle of the night is the surest way to guarantee you don't get another wink. I had started by analyzing the crease in the pillow that ran like the San Andreas Fault under my cheek. As I obsessed over the state of my pillow, I methodically worked my way through a checklist of physical indicators to determine my current state of health.

"Is my spine intact?" I asked myself. "Will my ear stay this way, folded in half under my cranium? And what's that? Is that where my bladder actually resides?" Oops. Thought about it. Now I would have to get up and do something about it. I yanked on the covers and did a quick evaluation of my dark surroundings. My brave offer to take the side of the bed nearest the door had gone unnoticed, but you never know when you'll have to defend your family against marauding motel hooligans. I lay still, and listened as the pipes in the wall at the head of our bed creaked and groaned, reminding me of the house I grew up in.

"Ignore it," I told myself. I listened to what I thought was the heater humming in the other corner of our motel room.

"Is that the ocean?" The ocean stopped humming for a moment, changed gears, and picked up again.

When I could no longer deny that my bladder was wide awake and ready to start the day, I rolled silently out of bed and padded cautiously across our pitch black double-queen non-smoking room towards the flimsy curtains that kept guard over our third story ocean view. I peered into the mist as the waves pounded against a pre-dawn beach thirty-five feet below me. I couldn't see any ocean really, just the ghostly whitecaps of the Pacific as it collided with the ocean floor and stumbled onto the sand. Across Puget Sound a thin pale brush stroke stretched from north to south across the dark sky. Soon the glorious, warm hues of daylight would overtake the darkness above and the darkness below. It was Wednesday, and I was officially awake.

With nothing else to do as long as my family lay sleeping, I set up a makeshift desk on my lap in the motel bathroom, and began reading and taking notes. After months of wondering if I might be the only Christian questioning my anti-evolutionist roots, I had recently picked up a copy of *Saving Darwin* by Karl Giberson. The title was controversial enough for my liking and I had grabbed the first copy I could find. The premise of *Saving Darwin* is that the creation/evolution debate that has raged in North America for the past 120 years is not a scientific debate at all, but rather a war of culture, a war of ideas.

Giberson's account of the antagonism between the Church in North America and the scientific establishment made me feel less anxious about my unsteady state of faith. I felt my shoulders relaxing as I turned the pages.

I read and pondered, scribbled a few notes and read some more. I didn't know if I'd ever be willing to believe in evolution like Karl Giberson, but at least I had found a friend, a resonant voice as I wrestled with my own questions about the role that my faith could actually play in a society tuned in to facts and skeptical of dogma.

On one hand, I was still convinced that faith in the God of the Bible was bound, eventually, to intrude into the lives of intelligent, educated people. But I was also feeling guilty at how evangelicals, the community of faith I'd grown up in, had managed to cultivate such a hostile attitude towards people steeped in a scientific worldview. "Where is the love, and grace?" I asked myself. Where are the warm gospel fuzzies that are supposed to attract a hurting world in need of answers?

Where are my legs?

By this time I'd been holed up (literally) in the bathroom of suite 328 at the Aladdin Motel for over forty-five minutes, with pen in hand and boxers around ankles.

In the process of studying this dangerous Christian writer and then pouring my heart onto the pages of a blue coil notebook, I'd forgotten that the elliptical orbit of a toilet seat will eventually cut off all circulation to one's lower extremities. It happens every time.

I knew that if I remained seated and continued reading I would finish chapter five before the sun rose, but I would likely never walk again. If I put the book down, however, it might be possible to drag my lifeless legs with upper arm strength alone across an expanse of linoleum to the bathroom door, about six feet away, and beyond into the carpeted darkness. If I had any hope of arriving, in muted agony, back in my bed, *Saving Darwin* would have to wait. There were some important parts of me that I had to save right now.

For the next several minutes I crawled and eventually shuffled along the wall of our motel room, inch by tortured inch, until, propped up against the sliding glass doors like a two-legged easel, I found myself staring into Puget Sound. The black Washington sky was now bleeding tangerine through a ragged horizontal tear above the bay. Sunlight and the promise of a new day in the Wray family with only half a dad loomed large. I panicked, knowing that if I failed to get back into bed before the compulsory crackling of nerve endings ensued, my wife would awaken to the whimperings of a waffling closet evolutionist, pinned to the window by his own limbs in the first documented case of self-paralyzation by toilet seat. I continued my slow, deliberate journey towards the bed. As the first treacheries of circulation engulfed my gluteal region, I reached into the darkness, flailing for something solid to hold onto. I think that's a television. I steadied myself. My hand brushed across the screen.

In a twist of divine proportions, a parade of pins and needles started their dance of joy in my upper legs at the exact moment a glowing, sizzling stream of blue and white sparks began to fly, arcing between my outstretched finger tips and the TV screen.

My foot dragging across the motel room carpet had turned my semi-anesthetized mortal coil into a lightning rod. And this thirty-two inch Sanyo, the only piece of furniture in this room preventing me from becoming another pile of motel room laundry, had morphed into a Vander-Graph generator. I stood still, but fully charged—suspended between the dark of night and the brilliance of dawn, between hope and losing faith—a captive audience to the miniature lightning storm playing out between my fingers and the silent black box.

The ancient Germanic tribes believed that the hammer of God was the cause of thunder. The Aztecs believed the deities would smash their water jugs together to terrorize the earth. Still other ancient tribes, convinced that the thunderous curses of an angry god signaled the launch of lightning bolts from his heavenly throne, would cower in the face of the storm, pleading for mercy. I, on the other hand, have a sneaky suspicion that God simply enjoys shuffling his sock feet across a really big carpet. Just to see the light show.

26
ASTRONOMY 101

Fifteen minutes west of the Okanagan Valley in British Columbia, where we spend a week every year camping and baking in the summer heat, sits the Dominion Radio Astrophysical Observatory (DRAO). I had known it was there for several years, a few miles off the highway, collecting dust in the collective consciousness of almost every person in this valley except for its few dozen employees. As the kids were now old enough to stake out their own territory at the beach, I packed up my camera and made the thirty minute drive into the hills to see what all this astrophysical observing was about.

The main task of DRAO is to observe the radio waves being emitted by the hydrogen gas particles in our Milky Way galaxy. If it isn't supernova or something immediately impressive, the Galactic Plane Survey, as the project is officially known, collects and analyzes the data. The information being monitored at DRAO is fed to astronomers all over the world who are attempting to learn more about the conditions of the universe shortly after the Big Bang. This all sounds impressive, but do these guys have a gift-shop?

After the twists and turns dotted with more than a few "Acreage For Sale" signs, the pavement opened up into a parched, yellow meadow. I felt a strange sense of wonder, like I was about to be let in on a very big secret. Even the words DOMINION RADIO ASTROPHYSICAL OBSERVATORY, detailed in 260-point type on a worn 4x8 plywood sign beside the road, lent an ominous sense of adventure to this otherwise sleepy valley strewn with conifer pines and wild grass. A smaller sign instructed me to turn off my cell phone, and leave my car at the gates. It would be a four hundred meter hike into the observatory.

As I locked up the car and pulled on a ball cap to ward off sunstroke, I took note of an ugly collection of clouds that was forming on the north side of the valley. The wind had been intense since I got out of the car to read the information board, and I was already bristling at the chill in the air. It was a welcome change from the 102 degrees I had endured the day before. As I reached the top of a short incline on the roadway in to the compound, I reached a series of white radio-wave dishes—about five stories high. (These were the little guys.) It was eerie, and awesome. So far, I was enthralled with everything about astrophysics and I was barely out of the parking lot.

The wind picked up again.

As I knelt on the asphalt to get my camera out of its bag, a sudden gust of wind sent me sprawling onto my side. I swiveled around and found myself dizzy, hunkered down on all fours, clutching at the ground as though gravity was about to expire. My bare knees, scraped and bloody, would have to wait. I reached for the strap hanging around my neck and scanned my new Nikon. It had never touched down.

I gathered my feet under me, and stood defiantly. Like Gandalf in the Mines of Moria, I took aim at a two-story brick building across the valley. The wind continued its assault on my eyes and ears as I staggered along taking slow deliberate steps. To the casual observer, it probably looked like I had stepped out of the bathroom after reading for forty-five minutes. I clung to my hat, praying another gust of wind wouldn't launch it into the long grass beside the roadway where I knew a brood of Okanagan rattlers would be in waiting.

Even though I was able to keep my feet, the wind howling across the small plain directly into my face was deafening and more ferocious than I had ever encountered. I could barely exhale against the gusting. My nostrils were fluttering like windsocks on a prairie landing strip. I considered the shame it would bring on my family if I became the first person in history to drown in air. I decided that walking backwards might be the best way forward, but after a wheelbarrow load of pinecones screamed by me at a velocity and altitude that would have surely left me welted and earless, I turned once again into the storm, on guard against incoming forest debris.

And I was doing this for what? I wasn't exactly sure yet. But I could tell by the abundance of chain link fencing that surrounded the perimeter of this compound that I was, at the very least, about to discover the final resting place of a few hundred million dollars of Canadian tax revenue.

Moments before I froze to death in a desert valley in the middle of July on my summer vacation, I reached a small collection of buildings huddled under an older and much larger dish structure. I spotted a sign on one building that let me know it was the Visitor's Centre. I dashed for the door.

"So this is what it feels like to arrive at the South Pole," I trumpeted as I marched confidently into a sparse room that contained exactly... no one. Apparently tour guides wouldn't be available until the weekend, when they would answer questions and treat frostbite. But today I was on my own. I couldn't even reserve a team of dogs to guarantee a safe return to my Subaru.

Enjoying the silence and warmth of the indoors, I took a moment to gaze around the room. It was not much bigger than an elementary school library. The walls were adorned with large murals, text and photographs. A couple of bulletin board displays were set deliberately in the middle of the room next to a guest registry and a wooden bench. The front gates of Cape Canaveral this was not.

For the next ninety minutes I was able to traverse every linear foot of wall display that framed the hall. I read about cosmic background radiation—the noise that a universe leaves behind after it explodes into existence. I read about radio waves, which are much longer than infrared or visible light waves. I read about gamma rays, which are shorter still. All I knew about gamma rays was that a large majority of comic book heroes hadn't treated them with any respect. But radio-waves, which can be anywhere from several centimeters to a few meters long, can travel millions of light years (600 trillion miles per year) across the galaxy, and pass through our atmosphere in every direction. Some of them were being intercepted right now, picked up by the five-story satellite dish outside on the observatory lawn (if the science can be believed).

If, because astronomy, as it is presently taught and accepted by most people, is necessarily suspect when viewed through the creationist lens, a sincere young earth creationist cannot, on one hand, believe that the earth is less than ten thousand years old, and on the other hand believe that this so-called science is good for anything more than blatant fantasizing. All this technology, the signal processors and synthesis telescopes calibrated to record images from the heavens, are useless in the grand scheme of things because, according to the creationists, God didn't actually put the universe together in a way that we could comprehend or measure. He only made it appear that way.

For a creationist, the only thing to be taken seriously in the maze of this expensive gadgetry is a hypothetical question: Why does the universe appear to act in this way? It's an eerily similar question to the one posed by skeptical clergy in Galileo's day. The answer is that God makes the universe appear to act in this way because he is testing our faith. In the mean time, we can play at cosmology and quantum physics if we wish, or throw around silly ideas about curved universes or deep time, but we can't actually believe that the universe is like this at all. Especially if a team of technology addicts on a hill outside of town claims to have inside information that doesn't involve Scripture.

According to the creationists, the light from the Andromeda Galaxy didn't really travel 2.5 million light years before entering our retinas, because the Andromeda Galaxy isn't that old. Obviously God must have created the universe with the light already "in transit." Why has the math never been contested? Or the speed of light? If the Bible really is the authority on matters of cosmology and particle physics then it stands to reason that the speed of light and Albert Einstein's famous little equation are to blame for much of the confusion in our fallen world. Perhaps it would be more productive for the creationists to overturn $E=MC^2$ and recalibrate our universe down to more manageable, biblical proportions. Better to keep the math simple than to insinuate that God's universe is strung together with counterfeit chronology.

What the creationist is implying, without ever saying it aloud, is that centuries of observation and calculation must be tossed aside to make way for Genesis, the de facto handbook of cosmology to the ancient Hebrews.

We know about the Hebrew view of the cosmos from the Old Testament as well as other sources. They believed the earth was flat, and the stars over head were held in place by several layers of crystal spheres. They understood the firmament (spoken of in Genesis) to be a solid surface, able to keep water from cascading onto their kibbutzim. The ancient Hebrews were convinced the four corners of the earth were exactly that—corners of a flat surface resting securely on the earth's foundation. Think of a snow globe and you're getting close. Their poet-hymn writers talked about storehouses laden with snow. We know there aren't any. It still makes for great poetry, but we don't get all worked up over the imagery. We don't take it literally, even though the Hebrews may well have. A twentieth century explanation of snowfall would have been as useful a gift for a first century synagogue library as a recipe for lemon meringue pie.

I believe that God's chosen people were chosen for a very good reason, but I don't think it was so they could leave their cosmological footprint on human history. The ancient Hebrews did not have the slightest inclination towards measuring the cosmos. You have to remember, it took the Israelites forty years to complete a three week hike to the Promised Land. Accurate surveying technique was beyond the grasp of these people. For a Hebrew waiting to enter a land flowing with milk and honey, the brainteaser of the day usually involved finding ways to stay alive longer than your goat.

The first book of Moses was never intended to explain the "what" of the heavens and the earth. God knew that with time, and a toolbox of increasing complexity, we'd come up with many of those answers on our own. The "why" of creation, however, was definitely a mystery worth sharing, and Yahweh chose to share that secret with the Hebrews.

It turns out there is no gift shop at DRAO. That's probably not a bad thing, because I didn't see a single gift shopper all afternoon. What was even better was that I didn't see any Okanagan rattlers or flying pinecones as I made my way back to the parking lot.

§

One summer night I found myself sprawled on a rickety lakeside dock staring up into a sparkling night sky. I was enthralled with the bigness of the heavens and the smallness of my own understanding. The guy sitting next to me suggested that the stars were put there for art, not as "timepieces."

He said it matter-of-factly, the same way you tell your mother that her dress is tucked into her pantyhose. He was implying that our methods of measuring the temperature of a galaxy or its cosmic nearness is hopelessly flawed because the Bible rules out the idea of great big bangs and millions of light years.

Just as Galileo mourned over the devout naysayers who refused to sneak a peek through one of his telescopes, lest their eyes become blinded to the truth of God's word, I found myself mourning for a friend who hadn't allowed enough space in his life for a really, really, REALLY big God.

27
DEEP TIME

In the world of humans, we order our lives by the ticks of a clock or the jingle of a text message. In the world of humans, we measure time in minutes and hours. The rotation of planet earth takes twenty-four of these hours. Every 365.25 days, we complete a single orbit of the sun, the nearest star of the 100 billion that call our galaxy home. We've been keeping track of time like this for a while now. We know no other way.

Not long after man learned to communicate and build and hunt and farm, time became a challenge. Then somebody invented the iPhone. In our efforts to master the intricacies of the handheld digital device and improve our ability to communicate, we ran out of time to accomplish anything else. Farming and hunting are largely ignored these days. Something had to give. But this "time" as we've known it isn't deep time. Deep time isn't like any other time and, well, for creationists deep time never happened. Shallow time is all we've got to account for everything we see before us. When one is trapped in shallow time, however, on a planet only six to ten thousand years old, certain details are cause for some serious head scratching.

Continental drift, for example, refers to the physical movement of the earth's tectonic plates over the surface of the globe. North America is gliding away from Europe and Africa at the leisurely rate of two centimeters per year (less than an inch) if you believe the people who measure these things. What this means is that in 1492 when Columbus crossed the Atlantic in search of the new world, his journey was about four feet shorter than it would be today. This may explain a slight increase in twenty-first century cruise ship fares, but I smell price gouging.

While uniformitarian geology allows for slow change over hundreds of millions of years, thus saving the Santa Maria less than a single tick on the odometer, some creationists have suggested that Pangaea, the supercontinent which existed before our late model continents broke apart, must have split into fragments during Noah's flood—about 4,300 years ago, and that the continents came to rest in their current positions only a few weeks after the Genesis flood had subsided.

To understand what this looks like in real time, one only has to do the math. For Florida to go from a standstill to sitting 4,600 miles off the coast of Spain in, say, forty-six days (let's keep the math simple) Europe would have to be separating from North America at an average of... 100 nautical miles per day. What would this look like? Close your eyes and imagine wakeboarding behind Portugal.

28

A WALK IN THE PARK — PART 3

T he sun had been dodging in and behind the clouds for most of the morning, warming my skin but not threatening to leave a burn. My first full day as a paleontologist was going better than expected. I knelt on a foam pad, my neck shielded by a borrowed Tilley hat. I was staring intently at a mesmerizing piece of dirt.

I had been instructed to "trench" around the partially buried vertebra, about eight inches in diameter, sitting before me. Not just any vertebra. This was centrosaurine vertebra. And not just a coddle—one of the tiny tail pieces, or a cervical vertebra—from the grouping of bones at the base of the skull that fuse together to support the weight of a massive skull as the creature matures. (I had learned all of this only this morning.) No, I had been charged with the task of extricating a centrum vertebra—one of the largest, knobby looking pieces of bone found in the spinal column.

Twenty minutes earlier, Marie had carefully pointed out the lateral processes, tiny nubs on the sides of the bone, which, according to well-established principles of anatomy, signify proximity to cartilage and ribs. Several ribs, all at least fifteen inches long, lay encased in sandstone less than two feet away. Every one of these fossils had already been mapped and tagged, catalogued in a database linking the whereabouts of each one in relation to a stake hammered into the ground at the edge of our dig site. This single bone could be identified using GPS technology. It might be months or even years before all of these bones were pulled out of the ground, but every paleontologist associated with this dig already knew where every valuable piece of the puzzle was situated.

My job this afternoon was to remove the excess sandstone from around the edges of fossil, and work my way carefully underneath it, exposing as much as possible, while maintaining the support under it. When this trenching was complete, the bone would be capped with gypsum, in a plaster cast, to keep the fossil intact when we pried it out of the ground. Only two hours ago I had watched wide-eyed as Marie carefully planted a small geologist's pick under the already capped forearm of an adolescent centrosaurine. Gently, almost reverently, I cradled the plaster-encrusted fossil in my bare hands as we rolled it over, exposing the underside.

I had just flipped my first ulna.

This was slow work, but life couldn't get any better. Here I was in the twenty-first century, the age of titanium hip replacement surgery and chicken tandoori pizza, down on my hands and knees attempting to finesse a dinosaur fossil out of the side of a mountain with a dental pick.

"We are not going to finish this today, are we?" I grunted to Beverly and Marie as I scraped away the sediment. They were also on hands and knees, capping a second, larger ceratopsian fossil in wet plaster. I went back to my sacred work, leaning into the vertebra as piece by piece the sandstone broke away.

"Uh-oh…" I heard someone say after I got too aggressive with a chunk of obstinate sandstone. Was that my outside voice? Marie had told me to call if anything went sideways. I offered up a desperate, quiet prayer. A more panic-induced Hail Mary has never escaped the lips of a practicing Protestant.

"Was that a good uh-oh or a bad uh-oh?" Marie had heard my outburst.

I stared solemnly at the biggest hairline fracture I'd ever seen. The only hairline fracture I'd ever seen.

"Well…" I fought for words. "Here's the good news. He was already dead."

"You'll have to wait a minute. We've got wet plaster over here," Marie called out, irritation evident in her voice.

I looked down at the shattered fossil, a wonder of God's creation, treasure of science and convincing evidence of deep time. This relic had survived in this exact spot wholly intact, protected from the prying claws of prehistoric scavengers, entombed in a sandstone sarcophagus, sheltered from the relentless forces of erosion and the savage rays for the sun for 76.2 million years. I had only been here since lunch... and I broke it.

29
DARWIN

I have my very own copy of *Origin of the Species* in my office these days and while I admit to reading it at less than breakneck pace (much to the dismay of my more conservative friends) what has surprised me the most is the lack of vitriol and despondency coming from the author as he lays out his relatively simple idea of Natural Selection.

I have also come to the conclusion that the laws of natural selection don't apply to authors. For all the impressive things he accomplished in his life—impressive enough to be buried at Westminster Abbey in 1882—spitting out page-turners wasn't one of Charles Darwin's strengths.

Yet, in spite of the book's plodding narrative, from the day his theory of natural selection landed on the streets of London, Darwin has been causing a stir on both sides of the faith/science debate. While evolutionary theory wasn't his invention (it had been simmering in scientific discourse for at least a century) the publishing of his work forced the argument out of the debating chambers and into the mainstream.

So, what exactly did Darwin do back in 1859 to get his mutton-chopped mug adhered to the dartboard in so many prayer circles? It had been twenty years since he completed his field studies before he unveiled his findings. And even then he was forced into action upon hearing that a competitor, Alfred Russell Wallace, was about to publish his own account of the same theory. The fact that it took him so long to tweak his manuscript indicates more than just a propensity for fact checking. Darwin was well aware of the controversy that would begin brewing once he went public. There has also been speculation that he was not sure of how his wife might react (for clarification reread Chapter 6: It's a Guy Thing).

While *Origin of the Species* had its fair share of critics within the scientific community and the church, it was not cast aside as the incoherent rambling of a madman. And while there are plenty of rumors that Charles Darwin had a deathbed conversion, biographers are consistent in their claim that his wife would have trumpeted any such recantations, as she held to her Christian faith consistently throughout her life and was distressed by the implications of her husband's research.

However, after Darwin's book was first published, many members of the clergy praised his findings as proof that an intelligent creator was at work in the universe. Adam Sedgewick, who had led the charge with his field study in geology, was a pastor, and had actually taught Darwin. Asa Gray, the American botanist stationed at Harvard was perhaps Darwin's greatest ally in North America. And he was a Presbyterian!

§

After joining the crew of the HMS Beagle as the captain's official traveling companion, Darwin quickly found himself fascinated by the diversity of species they came into contact with as they sailed down the east coast of South America. For almost five years, Darwin spent his on-shore hours wandering the countryside collecting specimens of plants, mammals, birds, insects and even fossils. He sent them back to England for further study. During the voyage and for twenty years after, before he finally published his most famous work, Darwin worked to frame a scenario that would give reasons for the distribution of species we find on our planet. Today we call this discipline biogeography.

Darwin's struggle was that he couldn't explain why the fossils of extinct species are only found in the same region as their living descendants. Sloths, rheas, platypuses, armadillo, kangaroos, lemurs, kiwis, ostriches, tortoises, etc. are all examples of species that Darwin studied in their specific, geographically diverse habitats. For example, species found along the East Coast of South America are closely related to species found along the coastal regions of West Africa. This makes some sense when you look at the map and realize that the two continents were at one time joined. The fossils unearthed in both locations show a pattern of similar species, or closely related ones in the same location. This same record of species distribution is true in every ecosystem and on every continent.

Darwin's musings, what we know as the theory of natural selection, simply state that those species best suited to survive in any system live longer, have more offspring and eventually become recognized as indigenous to that region. In fact, those creatures even look designed for their environment because they flourish within it.

One of the problems that creationists have with natural selection is that it does away with the traditional understanding of Noah's flood. (At least it was traditional in the untraditional evangelical world I grew up in.) If Darwin's understanding of species distribution across the globe was true, then the Genesis flood as it was commonly interpreted wasn't.

First of all, if the fossil record shows that the distribution of species follows a pattern of local migration only, then it is up to the creationists to bring forward evidence of global migration. If all animals were specially created by God at their specially designed habitat across the globe, and had to migrate to Noah's property, there should be at least some evidence to support this claim.

Furthermore it would follow that the eating habits of all these creatures would have been altered for the time it took them to migrate to the ark, and then back from Ararat. I suppose God could have changed the appetites of all carnivorous animals, turned them vegan for the journey, and he must have, for we have no fossil evidence that indicates such drastic movements of meat eaters into or out of the Near East.

Another possibility was that there was no death during this migration and all animals were kept alive until they returned to their natural habitat. Kangaroos, for example, would have traveled from Australia, over what is today the Antarctic (remember that on the young-earth timeline all the continents were joined together less than 4,000 years ago, right before the flood). Then they migrated north up the African continent, stopping for a drink at Victoria Falls, before bounding into the sands of the Arabian peninsula and onward to the Middle Eastern launch point of the ark.

All we are missing to make this proposition a full-fledged scientific theory is some evidence. OR it may be that the fossil record is astoundingly silent on this matter and scientists have failed to discover anything to support a global migration of every living species from its natural habitat to Noah. Which leaves creationists in the uncomfortable position of pleading with the fossil record for more evidence to support their position.

30

GLENN MORTON

I t seems that some people of faith have been able to reconcile biblical interpretation with Darwin's idea and still keep their theology intact. What I really needed about now was to talk to someone who had already been there.

C.S. Lewis was one of those people. Sadly, C. S. Lewis is dead.

Glenn Morton is also one of those people. Morton has been involved in the geophysics side of the oil and gas industry for almost four decades as a data analyst. His expertise has been instrumental in the discovery of thirty-four oil fields and has taken him all over the globe, including the high Arctic, the Himalayas, the North Sea and twenty-six different countries. He has lived in Beijing, speaks Mandarin and knows how to eat prawns the right way. I'm betting this guy could teach me something.

The other reason I wanted to track down Morton was because he was the ghostwriter for Josh McDowell's book *Reasons Skeptics Should Consider Christianity*. He penned the chapter on evolution. During that same time he also contributed over twenty articles to creationist publications before he pulled away from the discussion to rethink the evidence. While his talent at processing geologic data has proven very valuable to oil investors, he informed me that he has lost his edge when it comes to discussing science and faith.

"The only thing I can say," he told me, "is that if my theory isn't correct, isn't somewhere in the ballpark, than I have absolutely no idea of how to put any of this together. I'm tired of beating my head against the wall; I've said all I can say, I'm getting rid of my books. Nobody wants what I am offering, and that's okay."

I can't tell if I've caught him on a good day.

I was hoping to meet Glenn at his ranch so I could ask him about his new perspective on the origins debate. And I wanted to see some of Texas. But since his oil consulting business made it difficult to plan too far in advance, and I needed to book a cheap flight, weeks ahead, we opted for the good old-fashioned telephone interview. I was driving when we connected, so I pulled up to the curb next to a neighborhood park, turned off the engine, and grabbed my notebook.

"So you were doing an interview for the Wall Street Journal?" I asked, referring to an email from earlier in the day.

"Well, not really an interview," he said with more than a hint of Texas in his voice.

"They call me up every once in a while, and I give them my opinions on the state of the oil industry. I don't really get quoted. I give them status reports. That's all. I'm supposed to be retired."

He asked me what kind of project I was up to, and I told him straight up that I was working through the creation-evolution puzzle, and wanted to know more about his journey.

"When did you come to the realization that creationism wasn't cutting it?" I asked him.

"Oh golly... that was a twenty year struggle. I was trying to determine whether or not I was going to become an atheist. It all began in '85 and ended in 'bout 2003."

Okay. Spill your guts already, I said to myself.

"Explain what you were going through," I said to Glenn.

"Here's the thing..." said Glenn before taking a breath. "I still believe that if the Bible cannot tell us anything factually true about creation, then I don't see how it can be the word of God. Because that implies, in my mind at least, that God knows nothing about what happened. So he is simply Plato's demiurge. And that's not good enough for me."

First Atheism. Now Plato. Shut up and let the man talk.

"When I began to realize that creationism wasn't fitting with any of the evidence—that would have been the late 1970s—I was about three years into a project for Atlantic-Richfield processing seismic data. I wasn't interpreting the data, so I didn't need to handle the geology, just the physics and math, things like that, to process the data."

"You were already having some doubts?"

"Oh, yes, I mentioned to my wife about Henry Morris [founder of the modern Creation Science movement] and his inability to properly explain anything in geology, and she looked at me with a two edged sword and said, 'Do you have anything better?'"

Glen started laughing. I relaxed the grip on my pen.

"So, I tucked my tail between my legs, wandered back into my office and started thinking about that. So really, I knew from the late '70s, even before I began my young earth creationist publishing that there were severe problems with what was being put out there in front of people. All of my articles in the Creation Research Society Quarterly were aimed at trying to provide some explanation for what I was seeing in the real world data. But I became absolutely convinced that I had no explanation for that data. So, for three or four years I didn't publish anything. That was extremely unsatisfying. Then, I got laid off in 1986, largely because I was a young earth creationist."

"Because you were a young earth creationist?" I wasn't sure I had heard him correctly.

"A lady who had worked for me told the VP at Atlantic-Richfield I was a creationist. He said 'Well, he can't be any good as a scientist,' so I was shuffled off to another department until the next round of layoffs. And then I was gone."

"Did you find yourself angry with God or the Church or the Evangelical community?" I asked.

"No, I wasn't mad. I'm still not. I am sad for people who teach their children things that are liable to send them off to become atheists. But on the other hand, freedom requires that we have the freedom to be wrong."

My pen hadn't moved since Glenn started talking. The flashing red light on the digital recorder propped up in my console cup holder was a welcome sight.

"You see," said Glenn, "I have the freedom to try to talk people out of their creationist beliefs and they have a right to believe it. You have a right to believe whatever you want—even if it's the tooth fairy! As I continued to publish articles, I was methodically pushed out of the creationist movement. They wanted little to do with me, because I was talking about the issues that they didn't want to talk about. Some friends of mine said, 'Hey, go solve the problems' but everybody else wanted me to shut up, and eventually they got an editor in there that wouldn't publish any of my papers."

I could sense the resignation in his voice.

"I know you're saying that people have the right to believe what they want," I said, "but what is it about the geological facts that allows for such divergence of opinion?"

"Most of my career in the oil business has been spent judging the quality of scientific work, and it is amazing how much crap I find. And then when I speak up and say 'This fact and this fact and this fact over here don't fit your theory of where the oil is,' people have a tendency to ignore it.

"So what you're saying is that people only hear what they want to hear."

"Evolutionists do it. Investors do it. Even Christians do it. Because that is what every human being on the face of this planet does. You see, we all get into this group bubble. We are not objective. We think we are. The danger for each of us is that we operate on 'confirmation bias.' We spend our time looking for things that confirm our already established opinions. It's fascinating. And I'm not immune to it. Neither are you. We all think we're objective and we're not. We're just not."

My eyes wandered up and over my dashboard to a tangled mess of blackberry bushes thirty paces into the park.

"Listen to me," said Glenn. "I've struggled with the notion of becoming an atheist. I've got a son who's a preacher, and I actually told him at one point, 'I'm thinking about giving all this up.' My wife called me at work one day, and I said off-the-cuff 'I have something I want to talk to you about. Something important,' and she said, 'You're about to become an atheist, aren't you?' 'Not yet.' That was my answer." Glenn laughed again. He seemed to be having a jolly time with his indecision.

"So you don't believe creationism anymore, but you're not sure about the alternative?"

I already knew from his website that he is convinced that the Bible is the inspired word of God, written to all ages—ours included. But he has also faced the realization that while Genesis may be far from scientifically exhaustive, it does offer some statements that must either be true or false. Genesis 1:1 states, "In the beginning God created the heavens and the earth." This statement cannot be theologically true unless it is also factually true.

"You know, in some respects I think the creationists have it right," he said with a sincere tone.

"If Genesis doesn't tell us something historical about creation, how do we know we're getting anything else right? Any of the Jesus stuff? The liberals on the other side don't believe it in any sense. They say Genesis is nothing but fairy tales. But they still believe it because all the theology is true? Now… on what basis…" I could hear the twang rising to the surface. George W. would be proud.

"…On what basis should we say that the theology is true? How do we know the theology is true if none of the facts are? If every scientific fact in the first three chapters of Genesis is crap, why believe Christianity anyways? I don't see any reason to disregard something that's total nonsense in Genesis and still decide to believe the theology because I want to!"

"So where does that leave us?" I asked.

"Thankfully, salvation isn't based on what you believe about Genesis. But I think both the liberals and the conservatives are destroying the underpinnings of the Gospel." I was listening intently. My confirmation bias meter was beginning to hum.

"…One side has made Genesis untrue by tying it to an absolutely untrue and untenable theory. That's creationism. And the liberals make it untrue by doing the opposite. By declaring it factually untrue but theologically correct. Myth. They say, "'Oh yeah, the Genesis story is untrue, but there are a lot of life lessons in there. If both major camps in Christianity trot out a faith position that makes Genesis irrelevant, why should anybody pay any attention?"

31
WHAT'S NOT TO BELIEVE?

I must admit that I am a sucker for conspiracy theories, and there is none bigger, according to many evangelicals, than the hoax of evolution that is currently being perpetrated against our society. People who aren't believers can't get their heads around this, but it would be wise for those of us inside the community of faith to at least admit this much. We don't believe that the so-called experts are telling us the truth. But rather than allowing our fear of deception to drive us to investigate and learn more, we have systemically recoiled in the face of controversy. For people of the light, we sure seem to spend a lot of energy being afraid of the dark. It has become easy for me to talk about this with my agnostic friend Jack. I think he used to be an atheist, but now he's just agnostic. This might be progress!

Daring to speak out loud can often bring surprising moments of clarity, and Jack has become a sort of a sounding board—my personal atheist sounding board. Like using a tuning fork, I can put a voice to my thoughts on faith, and they bounce around in Jack's head for a few seconds, pick up a couple of free radical expletives and return to me for processing. Jack cuts right to the chase, and forces me to articulate. Like the other week, when I brought up the fact that a lot of Christians have some serious issues with the scientific community.

"Why are they so stupid? What's not to believe? It's just science."

"No, Jack, it's not just science. It's the enemy," I said.

"The enemy. What do you mean, the enemy?" He looked at me like I had a third ear growing out of my chin.

"A lot of Christians simply don't believe that science has the story right," I said.

"Believe. That's the problem," Jack said, getting agitated. Jack does agitated well. "There's nothing to believe. It's just fact. Are you so caught up in your faith that you apply it to every topic?" I was tempted to reply. He went on, "I don't have to believe that the earth is four and a half billion years old. I know it because the technology that I used in the field when I was a geologist worked. The math worked. The physics worked. And it works every time because it's true. THEY might believe, but I know. That's the difference."

"YOU were a geologist?" I asked.

"Yup. Back in Poland. I worked on a rig for the geological survey. Analyzing core samples."

"You were a geologist," I repeated.

"Still am," said Jack. "But only in Poland. In Canada I am your loyal IT guru."

"Thanks," I said, "but I think I need a geologist right about now." And I continued.

"A whole lot of people within the Christian community just don't believe it. It's hard to explain," I said. "Remember when you explained to me all the theories about the plane crash in Russia when the Polish president was killed?"

"Yeah. What's your point?"

"Listen, you view the Russians through your lens of Polish national pride, and are convinced they are capable of doing anything to mess with the Polish people. Am I right?"

"It's not a lens of Polish national pride... Russians are lying ba***rds. No two ways about it."

"The enemy," I said.

"You got it."

"That is exactly how many Christians view the scientific community," I said.

"Really?" He cocked his head to one side like a puppy trying to compute, tilted his head back to level and looked at me from under the rim of his glasses.

"Yeah, and that's the tragedy. I know exactly how they... or we think because I'm one of them, sort of... almost... maybe not anymore."

"I bet they're not crazy about you either," said Jack.

"I don't really care at this point. What I'm more concerned with is that people like you, watching us from the outside, are being presented with a screwed up version of God."

"How so?"

"Well... if the God of the Bible that you've heard about actually created the world 6,000 years ago and has orchestrated this whole billions of years age thing with the dating methods, and the dinosaur bones, just to test our faith... and it never actually happened that way, well... why would you want to get mixed up with a God like that? He's a con artist and a liar. Doesn't sound like God to me. Sounds like the other guy."

"So you don't believe anymore?"

"Yes, I do believe. What I'm trying to say is this. If God wants to make himself known, and he runs the entire universe, then it shouldn't matter how far down you dig into the earth's crust or into the workings of a cell or even a molecule of DNA. You should always, without exception, if you're honest with yourself and the facts, always, ultimately, find God whether you've ever cracked a Bible or not. Throughout history, most people have not had access to the Bible in its present form. But they still had nature to lead them. The Book of Nature doesn't lead away from the knowledge of God. That is impossible."

"So the Bible isn't needed, you just live your life, be a good person, don't shoot nobody..."

"No, the Bible is true AND science is true. Think about it, if one day science is able to prove conclusively that evolution is true, what do you think that might do to people's faith?"

"Kill it, I suppose."

"You might be right." Heavy words. "But that's not a necessary outcome. For some people, belief in the God of the Bible is intrinsically tied to disbelief of the scientific method. It is a recipe for spiritual disaster. I should know. I'm a recovering creationist."

"Whoa! You're really into this." Jack chuckled. "Are you going to write about me in your book?"

"Yup," I responded. "But I'm changing your name to Alexander or something exotic like that. I wasn't sure you'd be happy with your real name being plastered all over the pages of my book."

"Go ahead and use my real name. I don't have anything to worry about. But you'd better change yours!"

32

THE PROBLEM WITH BAD DESIGN

I was going to title this chapter "Intelligent Design—Not So Intelligent," which would have been both confusing and inflammatory if taken out of context. My other option for a title was "William Paley's Universe," which would have made sense only to those who are aware of William Paley's famous argument for design outlined in *Natural Theology*, published in 1802. Like that one is on your bookshelf.

However, William Paley's watchmaker analogy has been the backbone of the creationist argument for over two centuries. It reads as follows:

"In crossing a heath, suppose I pitched my foot against a stone, and were asked how the stone came to be there; I might possibly answer, that, for anything I knew to the contrary, it had lain there forever: nor would it perhaps be very easy to show the absurdity of this answer. But suppose I had found a watch upon the ground, and it should be inquired how the watch happened to be in that place; I should hardly think of the answer I had before given, that for anything I knew, the watch might have always been there.[...] There must have existed, at some time, and at some place or other, an artificer or artificers, who formed [the watch] for the purpose which we find it actually to answer; who comprehended its construction, and designed its use. [...] Every indication of contrivance, every manifestation of design, which existed in the watch, exists in the works of nature; with the difference, on the side of nature, of being greater or more, and that in a degree which exceeds all computation."— William Paley, *Natural Theology* (1802)

Now if Paley's argument is such an important cog in the wheel of creationist reasoning, and if creationism as an accurate accounting of natural history doesn't hold up against evolution (and I'm starting to lean that way) then it stands to reason that Paley's argument must be flawed. "So the entire purpose of this chapter is to ruin the reputation of a man who has inspired thousands?" you say. Well, not exactly. I have no illusions as to his place in history. William Paley will be fondly remembered long after my star of authorship has fizzled out like a Roman candle planted upside down in week old kitty litter.

However, if Paley's watchmaker analogy is the lynchpin holding the intelligent design wagon to the creationist tractor then I'm sure it won't hurt to ask a question or two, to see how everything holds up under duress.

My question goes something like this: Is it fair to say, as Paley does, that the watch is designed, and the stone on the hearth is not?

It seems pretty obvious that the watch shows unmistakable signs of design, but that is because I view the watch from the same plane of consciousness as the watchmaker. Even though I am not a designer of timepieces, I have the same set of cognitive tools as any watchmaker. We can agree, more or less, on aesthetics, accuracy, quality of construction and the ability of said watch to do what the designer intended it to do. In fact, the major component of this or any design argument has to do with intent. Regardless of what I think the watch might be good for at first ignorant glance, it is within my power to discern the intent of the designer. I can converse with the designer. I can understand what considerations he took into account when he drew up plans for his creation, and process those intentions. And if I was knowledgeable in the science and art of watch making I could even pronounce judgment on the relative success or failure of his watch design.

My ability to communicate with the designer makes it easy for me to "understand" his design. On the other hand, if I were a raccoon, I wouldn't have the slightest notion of intent. I would only perceive that the watch is rather solid, movable, and doesn't smell or taste like much. Sort of like the stone resting beside it.

So in one respect, design is subjective. Or to put it another way: just because I cannot perceive design does not mean that design doesn't exist.

Let's take a look at the stone on the hearth. It doesn't seem to do very much. It sits there. I might use it to keep a stack of grocery store flyers from flying off my front stairs on a windy day. It might help me break into my neighbor's car, if I find myself short of change for the bus. Which of these activities was the stone designed to do?

I can make any number of guesses as to the ultimate purpose of the stone, but without talking to the designer, I'm simply guessing. This is not that place in the book where I ask if you've had a little chat with the designer of the universe to find out why you're here. My point is this: our ability to discern design at all is limited by our ability to comprehend the motive that exists in the mind of the designer.

So Paley's design argument is essentially a wash. Just because we can prove that the watch IS designed, doesn't mean we can prove that the stone IS NOT. Perhaps it wasn't. While my belief in a creative God leads me to believe that the stone must have a purpose, an intended reason for its existence, regardless of whether or not I am able to grasp what that reason is, I just don't know. But I can believe.

However, it is another matter entirely to suggest that because I believe in a designer, a Creator God that made everything, that I have to believe he made everything from scratch, *ex nihilo*, every time he decided to act in space and time. In the book of Genesis, the Hebrew word *bara*, which means "to create from nothing" is only used three times, the first in Genesis 1:1 where it says, in the beginning God created—*bara*—the heavens and the earth. For the remainder of the story in Genesis chapter one, a different Hebrew word is used to describe most of the actions attributed to God and his making of things. In Genesis 1:11, God told the earth to bring forth plant life. In verse 20, God told the oceans to bring forth life, before telling the earth to do the same thing in verse 24.

Glenn Morton, who after much soul searching, reversed his position on the origins debate, maintains that Genesis teaches evolution implicitly. As Morton says, "God spoke to the earth and told it to do what he had created it to do. Bring forth—what the earth was capable of doing all on its own."

149

While this perspective, derived from what some call a fractured understanding of Hebrew vocabulary, doesn't do anything to minimize the creative abilities of God, it has serious implications for both evolutionary theory and intelligent design.

However, as Richard Dawkins states in *Greatest Show on Earth*, some of the evidence of design that we see in our species doesn't necessarily reflect well on the designer.

Simply put, there are many details in human anatomy that haven't been designed as well as they could have been. This isn't blasphemy, simply a comment on a few of the curious details we find inherent in every human being.

Our appendix, for example, doesn't come with any instruction booklet, and to date the medical community hasn't figured out what to do with the tens of thousands that they extract every year in hospitals all over the globe. Statistics show that not having an appendix can actually make you healthier. What was God thinking when he designed our appendix? And where are the experts warehousing all of them now, in the event we discover a health fix that needs just one more part? (I'm not even sure if this book has an appendix.)

"It makes perfect sense the moment you forget design and think history instead," says Dawkins. According to people who spend their lives studying these matters, our bodies contain evidence that suggests a long history of adaptation. Our appendix may not be of any use to us today, but there is evidence to suggest that in times past, when very similar species survived on diets heavier in vegetative materials, the appendix was a vital part of the digestive process.

And there are dozens of other examples of bad design, none of which reflect poorly on God's aptitude at this design thing. It is the Bible Science guys that have painted us into this corner where we don't dare admit that our anatomy might be flawed, because that would suggest that God goofed up. If it is true that we are prisoners in a less than perfect body plan—one which breaks down, and eventually wears out—it is a body plan that according to the evolutionists, has endured for millions of years, surviving and adapting to every curve thrown at it. A temporary dust bucket, molded over time to house a human soul that would never wear out. And God saw that it was good?

33

VITAMIN C

If you were to meet me for the first time, you'd likely not consider me diseased, but I am. Something inside of me is broken. I've tried in vain to keep it in check, but just when I start to feel like I've got a fighting chance at success, the fragile balance snaps and I pull up lame, embarrassed at my own incompetence and flippant disregard for what I know to be true. A couple of days ago it happened again.

I caught a cold. I know it's not exactly like winning the meat draw at a fast-pitch fundraiser, but I was starting to wonder if it was ever going to happen. For the first time in almost eighteen months I'm wandering about with a box of Kleenex and a pocketful of citrus lozenges. To lessen the pain when I swallow, my cheeks have decided to contort as though the muscles in my neck have frozen mid-yawn. That's a different kind of panic, a whole new reason to find a doctor. But tonight all I really want to do, apart from sleep, is try to make some common sense out of the common cold.

For the last year and a half, I've been ingesting vitamin C in large doses, and had become convinced, while everyone within sneezing distance came down with something—twice over—that I'd finally found the secret to beating the common cold. At first I was a weekend pill popper, managing a habit of six or eight 500mg hits a day when I felt a cold coming on. But chewables are a gateway drug, and before long I had graduated to half-gallon jugs of orange juice. I considered going intravenous, but the pulp would have clogged up something vital.

So what is vitamin C and why can't the human body make the stuff internally?

Vitamin C, also known as ascorbic acid, is a naturally occurring nutrient that bolsters the immune system in our bodies and helps fight off free radicals. Free radicals, as their name suggests, are the Taliban of your internal chemistry set. These angry little cells contain a single electron, which usually means trouble, and are prone to appear when our food is converted to energy and our bodies are forced to interact with pollutants such as tobacco and pop-tarts. Vitamin C also increases the body's ability to absorb iron from the plant-based foods we eat. Vitamin C is absolutely necessary to our survival, and its scarcity has caused much grief.

In years past, merchant marines and sailors who would regularly spend months at sea, miles from the nearest juice bar, were highly susceptible to scurvy. When the body can't maintain a decent level of ascorbic acid it stops producing collagen, and connective tissues begin to break down. Once the Brits, or 'limeys' as they were called, started dragging barrels of lemons and limes aboard to round out their diet, scurvy retreated quietly into the history books.

Vitamin C is intrinsic to my wholeness, and yet no matter how desperately I wish for it, I am unable within myself to solve the problem. It doesn't seem fair that almost every mammal on the planet can manufacture vitamin C using an elixir of five enzymes produced in the liver, and I have to rely on the twenty-four-hour pharmacy and a bowl of fruit salad. Yet, here I sit in spite of the chicken soup, a broken man, red in nose and heavy in heart.

Forget about nearsightedness and the propensity of toenails to grow in the wrong direction. Forget that just last week I needed tweezers to extricate several hairs from smack in the middle of my forehead, and I'm the only person I know with an advancing hairline. If I were given the opportunity to be God for a day, the one small oversight in human biology that would become my first order of business involves finding a cure for the common cold.

I would retrofit every *Homo sapiens* with a tiny onboard vitamin C factory. It wouldn't be very difficult (if I were omnipotent) to cut and paste a fully operational piece of DNA from another body plan, let's say a goat (which produces about 20,000 mg of vitamin C every day) and drop it into the human genome. Now that would be intelligent design! Problem solved. Except for the fact we would see a spike in the unemployment rate of the guys who pour all the tiny colored balls into those non-drowsy caplets.

Imagine the things that we could accomplish if we could claw back all the workdays lost to cold and flu. Studies have found the common cold (a preventable illness if the human body had been designed intelligently) is responsible for billions of dollars in lost economic opportunity every year.

But wait. The human body already contains every single component required to produce vitamin C. As it turns out, the instructions for building ascorbic acid are embedded in our DNA. And four of the five enzymes required to complete the task are contained in our liver. Adding to the mystery of this design flaw is the fact that the fifth enzyme, lovingly referred to as GLO by biochemistry buffs, isn't missing from our internal inventory; it is simply dormant. This is puzzling.

Anthropologists have theorized that at some time in our past, human diet may have included so much vitamin C that our bodies shut down that function. I mentioned that almost every other mammal produces vitamin C internally. Members of the bat family don't. Guinea pigs don't. Which makes being a human guinea pig now more hazardous to your health—if you're testing cold medication. The only other mammals that don't produce vitamin C internally are also primates—chimpanzees, orangutans and great apes.

What is somewhat controversial is that according to scientists now studying the completed DNA record of chimps, they also carry the defective gene for making GLO in their DNA sequence. It is located on chromosome eight—exactly where geneticists predicted it would be, based on their mapping of the human genetic instruction book. Now it is entirely possible that what appears on the surface to be hard evidence of shared ancestry is really coincidence. (If I am allowed to back pedal and amend my to do list for the day I get to be God, I'd like to remove all that dormant DNA. It may not be junk, but it appears to be sitting idly, loitering really— in the genetic code of both humans and the other primates, causing nothing but grief.)

Apparently this unfortunate pairing of genetic factoids has caused a lot of confusion. The vast majority of experts who make a career in genetics have convinced themselves that there is a link of sorts between the two species. I'm relieved that I didn't discover this little tidbit when I was a hard line creationist. What is now only trivia would have been truly traumatic.

34

SHOW ME THE MONKEY

Contemplating the possibility that I shared even a hint of DNA with an orangutan helped make sense of a few things. Like last summer when I tried to spray sunscreen from a can onto my hairy legs and ended up looking like one of those silver-flocked trees in the display window of the Salvation Army Thrift store. A crudely designed spray can, however, is no match against a heavily carpeted biped. The twist cap at the end of a tube of SPF 60 was intelligently designed for opening with opposable thumbs, and a UV tragedy was averted.

But the notion that our species, *Homo sapiens*, might have more in common with the apes than rugged good looks and a penchant for picking lice out of the kid's hair is a non-starter for many Christians. Even while some creationists may admit that evolution might have been at play in certain family trees, when push comes to shove, we much prefer special creation or divine intervention as the only palatable explanation of our insertion into the creation story. It's a classic case of evolutionary NIMBY, or more correctly NOGIMBY—No Orangutan Genes In My Back Yard.

There are two major reasons for this fierce denial.

First of all, we have convinced ourselves that unless those paleontologists come up with a fossil that can officially be titled "The Missing Link" we aren't buying any of it. As if some fortuitous researcher in the field will unearth a monkey who literally died in the throes of morphing into something other than a monkey. The problem is this: evolution doesn't play out the way the Bible scientists on the lecture circuit would have us believe. Humans are not the descendants of apes any more than a Fronkey is the descendent of a frog and a donkey. Evolutionary theory doesn't claim that ANYTHING can happen if we give it enough time, chance and trips to the plate. What evolutionary theory does state is that humans and monkeys (along with all other living things) have a common ancestor somewhere in history. According to the theory, the only evidence we would ever find in the fossil record, if we find any at all, would be a creature that looks sort of like a monkey. And it would be found in geological strata that is older, or further back chronologically, than both modern apes and modern humans. The intermediate between humans and apes doesn't lie on a timeline between humans and apes. It lies further back in history where the lineage of the two species converge, like the branch of a tree where two small twigs join together.

As Grant Keddie at the Royal BC Museum stated so emphatically that day I sat in his office, "There isn't just one missing link. There are thousands of missing links." And he wasn't apologizing.

There isn't enough space on the planet to house and organize all the species that have lived and become extinct over the course of our history. The missing links are a puzzle and a blessing all at the same time. Unless we have a record of every species that has ever lived, missing links are exactly what we should expect. We may not have fossil evidence for every period of time, but the evidence that we do find runs in a continuous sequence with ancient forms and body types in older geologic formations deep in the earth, to more recent forms and body types appearing in the younger geological strata nearer the surface. Of course erosion and geologic shifting can alter the order in which we make our discoveries, but the basic chain of logic doesn't change.

The second reason we refuse to acknowledge any ties to this blasted ape isn't based on our distrust of science or our ignorance of the evidence at all (even though we have girded our collective loins with these two strains of contempt for several generations now). Our main opposition is purely theological in nature. When I read, for example in Psalm 8:5, "You have made them a little lower than the angels and crowned them with glory and honor," a biblical reference that indicates my standing in the celestial pecking order and then I wander over to the zoo and stand back while a posse of degenerate chimps proceed to fling poop at a busload of sixth graders, I can't help but feel the disconnect.

How can I rejoice as the Psalmist rejoices in our glorious place among God's creation, when those clowns on the Discovery channel won't stop telling me I am nothing more than a Congolese Bonobo in fashionable pants? But for the grace of God and a fistful of mutated chromosomes there go I.

It is deflating enough to admit that after all the sermons, and all the worshipful songs and all the tears of repentance, I cannot escape the fact that I am only a man. A frail man, agitated, and at odds with the prospect of being less than a god, however, it is another matter altogether to entertain notions of actual kinship with anything in the created order that can't brew a decent Americano. When Scripture suggests that I am an adopted child of God, asking if it is theologically possible that I am also a human animal, one among many animals in this garden, is a thought we dare not admit to ourselves or even worse, think out loud.

However, for anyone who takes the time to investigate, there appears to be more than enough evidence that points to humans descending from an ancestor that is also an ancestor to chimpanzees, gorillas, orangutans and bonobos. At this point on the conversation, the only theory being presented with any scientific veracity is evolution.

35

NOTHING TO BELIEVE IN

While I have always been convinced there is a creator, this belief that everything we see around us was first imagined by an omnipotent God is exactly that.

Belief.

Things I believe are true about the universe.

But belief as a way of knowing isn't the same as processing scientific data. Most of us would agree. The bigger question is whether this difference makes believing less real or worthy than collected, analyzed and processed knowledge? After all, we make most everyday decisions based on what we believe to be true by personal experience rather than by intentionally processing the data. Do you know what a raspberry tastes like? Do I know what a raspberry tastes like? How can we be sure that we are both experiencing the same sweet, tangy sensation? It is sweet and tangy, right?

In a world running hysterically away from the idea of absolute truth, how can I have any confidence that your sweet truth is my sweet truth? Do I need to wait for a published peer-reviewed summary of the chemical composition of a raspberry before I decide if my hastily drawn conclusions at first bite are legitimate? Shouldn't I consult a website a la Rotten

Tomatoes in search of fruit critiques from produce aficionados before I decide to go public with my unfettered approval of raspberries? Am I even qualified to comment on the wild variance in both taste and smell between berry and bacon until I have been awarded a Ph.D. in gustation and olfaction from a prestigious university? Are raspberries tasty because the data tells me they are or because I already "know" it?

On a larger scale, many of us find ourselves in a war between knowing and "knowing." Some of this knowing we call faith. We don't have the data, and we're not going to wait for it to confirm our suspicions. Occasionally, we even take action based on nothing but faith, which according to the Bible is proof that our faith isn't just a party line of dead, dusty platitudes or wishful thinking.

History is filled with uplifting stories of people who pressed on in spite of hardship because of their faith in God or an idea. Faith can be a powerful and inspiring force. However, faith in things that are not ultimately true has also led people to perform irrational acts and waste their lives in bizarre pursuits. What sets faith apart from empirical knowledge is that faith refuses to be muscled into a test tube or allow itself to be dissected on a stainless steel table. Faith is, by its very nature, less verifiable using principals of the scientific method than, say, science.

That's why they call it faith.

Evolution, on the other hand, isn't based on faith.

"Hold it right there," you might say, as I often did when faced with a scenario in which natural selection and apparently godless, random chance was trumpeted as the prime mover behind our primordial past. "It takes more faith to believe in evolution than it does to believe in God." Yes, that is what the creationists have been telling us for a few decades now. But biological evolution isn't based on faith. It never was. Yes, it's true that some individuals or groups have used evolution as an excuse for disputing the existence of God. To those people, evolution is a convenient crutch to lean on as they formulate their fanciful atheistic dream.

But evolution, like gravity, is a highly developed theory (think framework) that organizes an extensive catalogue of verifiable observations about the natural world and helps make sense of a whole lot of things. In the words of Theodosius Dobzhansky, one of our generation's leading evolutionary biologists, "nothing in biology makes sense, except in the light of evolution." And biology, like all of the other sciences, isn't based on faith.

I don't have to believe in evolution when I read that one of every five hundred whales is born with a hind leg protruding from its body cavity. These legs are not "leg-like" appendages. They are non-functioning, undersized, fully assembled legs that feature a full complement of joints, ligaments, bones, muscle tissue and sometimes feet and toes. Whales are, as the evolutionary story goes, mammals that returned to the sea. Every whale in every ocean has a pelvic apparatus that doesn't make much sense unless this hypothesis is true. While whale genetics is not a career choice I ever considered in spite of the fact that it's now a booming business, the experts, whom I have no reason to distrust, tell us that the instructions for hind legs are present in the DNA of every whale. Hind legs became expendable sometime in the distant past and don't fulfill their original purpose in whales who now reside exclusively in marine environments. But, every once in a while, a newborn whale enters life with a spare part it no longer has any use for.

These under reported details, which add to a constantly growing pool of evidence for evolution, are things we can simply know thanks to the efforts of the people who study whale DNA. It doesn't take faith to believe this stuff. Faith has a much higher calling.

I don't have to believe in evolution when I hear about FOXP2. FOXP2 is the name of a gene found in human chromosome seven and it contains instructions, which allow for, among other things, human speech and language development. Researchers in Britain came face to face with FOXP2 as they tried to solve the riddle of an extended family (identified as family KE) dealing with three generations of speech and linguistic difficulties. The interesting turn in this story is that researchers were directed to the FOXP2 gene by teams who were already studying DNA in apes. The primate researchers had discovered that the FOXP2 gene in the ape family (located on chromosome seven, exactly in the same position where it can be found in human DNA) is also dormant. As the gene in monkeys is turned off, researchers had a hunch that the same mutation had occurred in the DNA of the affected members in family KE. After more detailed examination of the affected DNA in family KE, it was proven that this had, in fact happened. The FOXP2 gene was turned off in the affected family members making it difficult for them to form sounds and even read and write certain letters. It is understandable why this particular thread of DNA evidence might lead some people to theorize that humans have some very old ties to the ape family. Move along folks. Not much to believe here.

I don't have to believe in evolution when I hear about a human baby being born with a tail. This is not a common occurrence and can be tidied up with surgery. No need to redesign the Pampers just yet. However, the genetic instructions for building all the vertebra required for a fully functioning tail is already a part of our DNA and every few years doctors witness the appearance of a little something we call an atavism. Atavisms are physical characteristics, which manifest themselves in species that have no further need of those "design features" (unlike the vestigial whale pelvis which is present in every whale).

Another example of a vestigial trait in humans can be experienced every time you are cold or suddenly fearful. Each of us has tiny muscles surrounding each hair on our bodies. When activated, these muscles make our hair stand on end. As humans we usually refer to them as goose bumps. Most of us don't have enough hair to make this maneuver, which also increases insulation or makes a frightened animal appear larger, worthwhile. If reading this chapter this "raises your hackles" you are witnessing a vestigial trait in action. Congratulations!

Another case in point would be the left recurrent laryngeal nerve. The recurrent laryngeal nerve (RLN) sends signals to my larynx and runs from my brain down to my heart before circling around and winding back up to my voice box. The corresponding nerve that controls the right side of my voice box, takes a direct route from my brain to my larynx.

I first learned about the recurrent laryngeal nerve system as I was catching up on comparative anatomy, a branch of science that investigates how the body plans of different species mirror each other, and speculates on how those species may have evolved from common ancestors. The experts in this fascinating field have discovered that the RLN runs directly from the brain to the gills in fish, while it follows a circuitous route, in humans. Because our heart and lungs are further from our brains, the nerve on the left side has lengthened—adapted—and now extends almost two feet longer than perfect design would have called for. The reason it reaches from our human brain down around our heart and back to our larynx is because it's stuck, or tangled up with arch of the aorta, and has no choice but to lengthen as the embryo develops. And what's more, this nerve follows the same pathway in every tetrapod (four limbed vertebrate) on the planet. Vertebrates are descendants of fish. Giraffes have an RLN that is over fifteen feet long.

Thanks fish!

The RLN connects the voice box to the brain and has no business meandering down around the heart and back again. Once I come to grips with the hard truth, the verifiable facts about laryngeal nerves that fit together like pieces in a giant jigsaw puzzle and begin to frame a larger picture, I don't have to "believe" in this piece of evolutionary evidence at all. There's no need to flex my faith muscles here at all. It's just a warm stringy fact. Once I understand that the recurrent laryngeal nerve system in humans is further evidence that my human body has historical ties to the body plans of other species, I have a choice to make. I can either lose my wits and run screaming from the building vowing to never let another scientific fact cross my field of vision, or I can accept the evidence for what it is, a scientific fact that needs to find a home in my Christian worldview. And I am free to conserve my faith for other things.

If human beings had been spoken into existence, created from nothing only ten thousand years ago, as the young earth creationists interpret Genesis, there would be no rational explanation for vestigial traits or atavisms or shared DNA mutations being a part of our genetic inventory. However, these uncomfortable peculiarities do exist. It's almost like we are souls wrapped in duct tape. Our human bodies are so riddled with evidence of adaptation that the most logical conclusion is that they have indeed adapted. This is all too new to me. I'm not yet comfortable with the notion that I don't have to expend energy trying to believe any of this. These are only facts, pieces of scientific truth that are not supposed to pose any threat to my faith. Perhaps I need to conserve my faith for the really big challenges.

While it might be tempting to flex my faith muscles while viewing evolution in the light of this modest sampling of evidence, my ability to resist fades to almost zero when I am confronted with warehouse after warehouse of other discoveries from the fields of biology, embryology, anthropology, archaeology, botany, paleontology and… and science. Okay science. All of it! It's everywhere. These people go to work every day, probably sit in traffic next to you on the freeway, and their job is to discover and uncover stuff. And they just keep finding more stuff. This evidence stuff is everywhere. In the dirt, in avian skeletal structures, in excavation sites of pre-human remains found in Africa, at the bottom of the ocean, in flu viruses, in my neighbour's aquarium, under my fingernails, even in my organic breakfast cereal if you caught me on a good day.

Scientific pursuit has blessed us with mountains of evidence that, while mildly impressive when considered alone, become a stunning display of knowable truth once the complementary facts, collected over several generations, are laid out before us, interwoven in an intricate tapestry that illustrates the history of interconnected life on our planet. In football they call it piling on. In science labs and courtrooms they call it conclusive.

Like my friend Jack says, I don't have to believe in evolution.

36

THE FIVE STAGES OF GRIEF
(MOURNING HAS BROKEN)

t was almost like grieving. Not for a person, but for a way of life. A worldview. As a creationist, I had always been plugged into my faith, and the reasons behind why I believed. But I also held firmly to an "us against them" mentality. But suddenly, I was now facing a scenario where it appeared that THEM were right and US were sadly mistaken. Who let this happen? It was a sickening feeling to acknowledge after almost five decades of schlepping my life around on this giant mud ball that I'd been cheated out of my divine right to have the best perspective on everything.

In the 1960s, Elizabeth Kubler-Ross did extensive research and developed what we commonly refer to as the five stages of grief. These five stages are denial, anger, bargaining, depression and acceptance. Whether it's the loss of a job, a marriage, a family member, a pet, or even your favorite fine-tip roller ball pen, these five stages seem to be common portals that most people have to go through in dealing with traumatic events. Using the Kubler-Ross model, I offer the following as a guide to assist other creationists, intelligent designers or literal translationalists who, like myself, suddenly find themselves dealing with the death of their familiar understanding of Genesis.

Stage ONE: Denial

This one should be familiar to most readers, as this is where the evangelical movement has been stationed for a few decades now. In my case, from the moment of that first conversation with someone who interpreted Scripture differently than I did, I found myself trying to reason the entire disagreement away. After deep introspection I was able to let the whole thing go by repeating to myself that simple, soothing, time-tested phrase, "He's an idiot." This kept me occupied for about twenty minutes until I realized that I'd inadvertently skipped right over denial into anger (stage two). So my advice is to get angry early and often. You can always circle back to denial once you're weary of praying for the souls of those reckless liberal thugs intent on messing with Scripture. There are so many things you can accomplish when you're wrapped up snugly in denial. You can toss aside some silly, over-rated skills like critical analysis, for example. Denial is a wonderful place to be. Ask any Cubs fan. Denial is also a useful position to take while you're weighing the consequences, trying to determine if you're committed to "follow the evidence where it leads."

Stage TWO: Anger

We've already touched on anger, but I'm not sure if enough Christians have really mastered this gift. According to Scripture we are supposed to bear one another's burdens, but I still run into too many believers who wander around as if that chip on my shoulder isn't partly theirs. The trick is to focus your anger on the source of the problem: scientists. They're the ones who are conspiring together to flush the faith of an entire generation into the abyss. To stay angry for as long as possible, never read any article in the press or online from scientific publications. These people will stop at nothing to get their point across. They will resort to evidence, mathematics, quantum mechanics and polyploidal speciation experiments and have even concocted entire realms of study including geology, paleontology, anthropology and biogeography to trick us. Now at some point, you'll run out of anger. You'll hit the angst wall, convinced there isn't an ounce of wrath left in your bones, and then you'll look across the room and discover that guy in the white lab coat isn't listening anymore. Which leads to the next stage.

Stage THREE: Bargaining

This is the stage that liberal theologians are most familiar with, and we evangelicals despise them for it! And being conciliatory sets a dangerous precedent anyway, so let's just move on.

Stage FOUR: Depression

Sigh. This is the place where you may start asking yourself if you're ashamed thinking what you're thinking. If you're an avid supporter of Slippery Slope theory, this is the place where you draw parallels between your shifting perspective and the dark cloud that swallowed Charles Darwin whole. You've been told that Darwin lost his faith after concluding that natural selection was responsible for the speciation of the planet. You were likely not told that the sudden death of his eleven-year-old daughter Annie might have been weighing on his mind. Experiences such as this are worthy of the depression and faith-swamping confusion that accompany them.

Stage FIVE: Acceptance

Well, let's not get ahead of ourselves. I may have chosen to acquiesce to this new reality, but I don't have to like it. There is so much of myself wrapped up in what I believe that to throw off such a comfy garment as recent creation leaves me feeling chilly. I'm going to need some new clothes. Denial and anger can only get you so far, and are limiting as evangelism tools. According to Elizabeth Kubler-Ross, stage five acceptance eventually gives way to exhilaration. We'll see.

37

DOUBT COMES TO TOWN

So that's it, then. They're right.
The scientists, those atheists. Darwin.
All of them.

Right after all.

It was too late to pretend I hadn't been bombarded with the most terrifying thought perpetrated upon any person who finds comfort in a life of faith.

It might have been wise to take off on a lonely walk and pray for a reprieve from an episode of theological suicide. Calling my pastor to ask for the church elders and zap straps might have been prudent, but I didn't have the energy to reach for the phone. Instead, I sat motionless on the couch, staring blankly into a dead TV screen. I didn't even reach for the remote. I didn't dare let myself be distracted, but at the same time I wanted to be anywhere but on that couch, thinking those dark thoughts. The realization materialized and settled heavily on my chest with a soft silent thud, thick and damp, hopeless as quicksand.

If THEY, the evolutionists, are right (or at least more right in their understanding of the facts than the creationists) how am I supposed to make sense of God? What if I exist solely as a result of random chance and at the discretion of some giant cosmic dice tossed haphazardly across the universe and gathered in by no one?

My brain was fraying at the edges. My faith, which had always kept me upright in the face of unsettling circumstances, sat teetering like an army of dominoes on a flimsy table. But there was no crash. No dramatics. Only a steady drone of dreary musings to keep me company throughout that day, and into the next, and the next.

Perhaps there is no God, I whispered more than once, hoping that by articulating it, I'd somehow drag the beast out of my head and into the daylight, where I could kick the crap out of it. But that didn't happen. Bleak notions were followed by others even less hopeful. Maybe I've been fooled by a transitory religious impulse, like a thousand generations before me?

I tried thinking positive thoughts. It had worked before. Okay, so if there is no God, I might as well cut to the chase. I didn't want to waste any more of this short life trying to make sense of a God that isn't even there. Surely I could find better things to do with my remaining years of abject mortal loitering than spend them in church. I tried to think of something worthwhile. I hadn't water-skied in years. It wouldn't exactly fill the void long term, but at least I could add a sexy teal speedboat to my line of credit without absorbing any guilt from the mounting debt. After all, it would be a waste of eternal separation from the notion of deity if I couldn't even enjoy deficit spending.

In the following days, the sobering ramifications of a world without God caught up to me. I noticed I was staring at my computer keyboard rather than the screen. I shuddered a lot. I thought about my kids, and their ultimate worth. Would it matter if they amounted to anything in life, or were happy, or succeeded or failed, or lived long healthy lives? Did it matter if they overdosed at age twenty-four on the wrong side of town? What about my wife and our friendship and vows to love each other, built on our joint commitment to having God in our lives? What about the people that I loved, or thought I loved, and all the other things I had considered important up until this point in my life that were rocking precariously on a thin ledge? What about truth and justice? There just had to be ultimate value in this life even if I'd done my part to make a mess of it all.

§

Faithlessness is not like any other feeling or emotion or way of being. It's more than a dejected nod from your consciousness to your gut. But at the same time, it's less than a powerful statement of principle. I think it's more like a place than anything else. A lonely but crowded, noisy yet silent place. A stage where you are the only actor, and there isn't any audience. But you wish you had a script, and even a tiny gallery to take notice of your mumblings and shuffling about. A few witnesses to sit quietly by while you, the only character, pace back and forth, under the glare of lights that offer little illumination and no heat, waiting for a plot that won't reveal itself.

Faithlessness is like a platform at a train station. I've never been on a real train to anywhere, but in Vancouver we have a transit system called the SkyTrain. It doesn't matter where you plan to end up, or who you'd like to meet, if you're going to take the SkyTrain you have to leave the real world of people and community and climb a series of cold ugly stairs. And then you wait on a big slab of concrete.

Once you're at the station, there's nothing to do but read advertisements that tell you why your life isn't what it could be. And you listen for the whirring of a train, any train that will remind you that this isn't your final destination. Sometimes the sign overhead blinks out a few words of red type, explaining that the train about to pull into the station isn't for you—the train you want to be on is still somewhere else. But that's not so bad. At least you can peer through the windows and wonder about the other passengers on their journey. Some are reading, some are chatting. Most are sitting staring at their own feet, thinking about where they will be in only a few short minutes, perhaps an aromatic fusion restaurant with friends, or at the kitchen table with a bowl of leftovers and a laptop. Some will be starting a shift behind the counter at Starbucks where they will spin lattes listening to the musings of Billy Holiday or Neil Young.

Some passengers hold your attention for longer than others, like the stocky South-Asian guy in a Seahawks jacket. This guy has no intentions of staying where he is at the moment. He is holding onto the chrome overhead rail with one hand and an iPhone with the other. He stares out the open doors of the SkyTrain right at me. Right through me. His lips are moving and he's smiling. He's telling his girlfriend that he'll meet her in twenty minutes and he's so glad he doesn't have to stay here staring at people who are going nowhere.

Losing faith is like standing at a train station realizing that you are going nowhere. You don't have a ticket; there is no map, or any overhead signs with blinking red letters that offer any helpful instructions. What's worse is that this platform, this cold, hard slab of existence, doesn't even have any tracks leading into or out of it. Apart from the advertising, the constant reminders that your life isn't what it could be, there are no comforting sounds or smells in this place. And once you've resigned yourself to the fact that the waiting exists in and of itself, your only option is to trudge back down the stairs to wherever you came from and deal with it. You're not going anywhere else. Anywhere else doesn't exist.

Is it any wonder that feeble prayers offered up at times like these don't seem to help much?

Where Are You?

Where?

Where is this place that you can be found?
This desolate crevasse in the expanse of the cosmos?

Where are you?

While many have claimed that you are everywhere,
right now "everywhere" is as captivating a creed to me as "nowhere."

Is "where" a place in time, perhaps?
Like when I was a frightened child or back when men
would break their backs
building cathedrals to imply your presence?
Was there a time when you were
and are no longer?
Have you ceased being found
or are you simply less obvious in this light
than you've been to other people,
in other times?

Where are you?

Are you?

Would I be more than a heartbeat removed from this discontent
if I gave up trying to pin you down on a map
and could settle my soul with the notion that you simply are?
Would I feel less alone, any less abandoned,
if there was no grand answer to where,
but only a hint that you are?
Beyond the reaches of my lofty imaginings
stirs a defiant, clawing, ever-clinging hope that you are,
And yet deep in the shadows where hopelessness feeds on delusion,
where dark dreams feast on tales
of an absolute power corrupting everything it touches,
also lives the fear that you are.

Where are you?

You?

You?

I know what it feels like to be me
and making peace with that ragged reality leaves me spent.
Did you actually think I'd have room in this life for you?
Any tools to deal with you?
Any strength left after pushing and dragging my tiny world around all
day long
to gaze heavenward and consider that the greater reality
allowing me to make headway at all
is you?

Where are you?

Please don't leave the answer up to me.
Because on the good days I can't hear you over the babble
and the busyness

and the blustering arrogance
that billows from these lungs like smoke
above the ruins of another shallow conquest.
And on the bad days...
On the bad days when there is no conquest to speak of
I can't hear your whispers over the sighs that spill from these parched
lips
like silent curses exhausted of their fury.

Please, please don't leave this up to me.
Because after all the wishing and the wanting,
the praying and the pleading
what will become of me or any of the people I love in this life
if you are always somewhere else,
but never right here?

If the answer to "Where are you?"
is not "Here"
—that answer, whatever it may be—
is the worst possible answer to the only question worth asking.

But,
if you could somehow find a way,
any way,
to get from wherever you are
to this tiny place
in space and time
that I call "here"

Well...

That would change everything.

38

THE BRIDGE

After a few long days and longer nights, as surely as the numbness had settled in, I began to feel the presence of something else. Something pleasant. In the valley of the shadow of death or faithlessness, or whatever it was, I reconnected with a feeling that almost resembled—wait for it—hope.

I had to admit to a growing sense that I was still bothered by the harshest realities of life. Bothered by injustice, and poverty, and a host of other imperfections that were undeniably an echo, or the anti-particle of something better. I would continue to be bothered because love and eternal worth and destiny and commitment and success and failure weren't contingent on any of this biological stuff that held my bones together and kept the evolutionists busy.

I discovered that I was looking for ways to care because caring was the surest sign that some part of me was more than just proteins and water. Somewhere inside of me, but not constrained by my physical shell were values injected by some other force. I couldn't get away from the assurance that something "Other" was behind all this emotion and soul and energy. And I believed once again, and more confidently than ever before, that

God was. (It was belief but at the same time it was more like knowing. Not the kind of knowing that comes as a result of tidy math gyrations or scientific observation. This kind of knowing is more like when you know you are in love. There's no need to wait for results from the lab to confirm what you already "know" to be true.)

And that was that. My dark season of wrestling with faith, or lack of it, had locked onto me like a thick, suffocating fog on a Tuesday right after dinner and had coughed up its final tired fur-ball of skepticism about a week and a half later, early on a Saturday morning as I was gassing up my old Toyota. No more wondering about a God that may or may not be there. I believed without any doubt that he was the only absolute YES in a broken-down world that was rotting and papered over with nothing but MAYBES. With a renewed sense of purpose, I realized that I had to focus on a bigger question. How do I move forward in a world where the evolutionists are right?

§

I pull a green plastic chair around a small table and settle down with an Americano and a brownie. I haven't been here for quite a while, but I like it. The railroad-crossing signal has begun sounding. A freight train is muscling its way into the valley. The screaming of steel wheels on the rails, and clacking of the tracks at the crossing is almost drowned out by a late September downpour. Yes, I'm at Wendel's again. This place is the nearest I've been to a sanctuary in weeks (Sundays at our church are too hectic to qualify as a day of rest).

Ever since the government dropped ferry service to the north side of the Fraser River, this place has gotten even quieter. And with fewer commuters trailing past my perch on the patio outside Wendel's Bookstore, the sense of tranquility has increased. A couple of years back, a major piece of bridge construction was completed a few miles downriver, making the four and a half minute ferry ride redundant.

As I ponder the new bridge that connects Fort Langley on the south side of the river with the city of Maple Ridge on the north, I see how some disconnected pieces of my life are beginning to make sense once again. The new bridge is an engineering marvel, especially to a guy who can't quite erect a garden shed without losing a limb. A few summers back, on the day they unveiled the new crossing, sixty thousand people showed up to walk the span, take pictures, listen to sixties cover bands and wolf down $4 ice-cream fudge bars. Never once did we concern ourselves with the highly stressed steel cables that stretched from the concrete towers buried in the river, cradling the bone white of the concrete bridge deck. All we knew was that two locations fixed on separate shores were now permanently attached.

I can feel my faith strengthening by the hour as I think about that bridge. It was like I had lived my entire life with only ferry service to take me from faith over to reason and back again. And now that I had dared wander into the chasm that separated the two, I had found solid ground on both sides that could support a connecting structure. I no longer had to float in the river, leaving faith on the one side, while I reached over to the shores of reason, never being able to trust one until I had let go of the other. For the first time the two sides of the river were connected and vibrant, like a synapse in the brain that has been re-wired by the adoption of a new habit.

I am torn away from my ponderings on the marvels of modern bridge engineering by the sound of singing. Behind me on the patio a couple of guys with guitar in hand are working over some lyrics and an inspired melody. Maybe I'm not the only one who comes to Wendel's to find God.

I don't think I'll be back here anytime soon. My daughter's dance class is moving across the freeway, and I expect I'll have to loiter in a nondescript strip mall not five minutes from that fancy new bridge, and chew on a milkshake straw or a side of fries while she works on her routine. My dance class snack habits will change. I'm not sure I'll hear God the same way either.

I wonder how easy it is to hear God in a strip mall, next to the freeway, lined up at the drive-thru. It's easy here at Wendel's when you're sitting under the propane heaters on the veranda, tucked away in a mythical hamlet where silence makes more noise than anything apart from the rain and the railroad tracks. Simple logic thrives in this lazy town, forgotten by the hyper-speed masses in their frantic commute into the city. Into the future where big town rationalism struts and crows. But there's no use in wishing for a simpler time when no one was in a hurry and there was no such thing as a conversation that went on too long. No use in pretending that technology hasn't triumphed and that internet chat rooms don't outnumber corner store bull sessions one thousand to one and that ear buds don't make it convenient to ignore any human that gets too close.

I'm sure he's there.

God.

On the other side of the freeway in the strip mall.

But I'm not convinced the pace of life in a drive-thru will make it easy to hear him. I suppose he could hang out somewhere between the order screen and the pick-up window, and tell me that it's not okay to have three butters with my blueberry bran muffin. That would be something that he might try. I suppose God will use whatever technology I'm plugged into to get my attention. Is it as easy to get somebody's attention as it used to be?

WWJT?

What would Jesus tweet?

39
FACING THE ANSWERS IN GENESIS

I broke from the norm yesterday and went to church on my own. Someone else's church. I drove east a few miles to a large church in the Fraser Valley, an hour's drive east of Vancouver. The Fraser Valley is the closest thing we have to a Bible belt in our part of the world. I had heard that Ken Ham, the founder of Answers in Genesis, would be speaking in the morning service to kick off a creationist conference. I'd been awake half the night tossing and turning, visualizing the conversation that might break out if I ever got a running start at the guest speaker.

I drove into the parking lot twenty minutes early, proving to everyone who knows anything about church attendance that I really was a visitor. After the initial uneasiness of spotting several women in floor length print dresses and long hair, a sure sign of extreme conservatism in our part of the country, my first contact with humans proved to be a friendly one. As I entered the foyer I could hear people milling about in morning conversation. I could smell the freshly brewed coffee. But I could hardly see a soul for the mountain of books and DVDs piled on tables all across the foyer like discount rice cookers at Wal-Mart.

After a careful perusal of the merchandise set before me, I considered heading to the car to fetch my camera, but reconsidered. That might be too obvious. I had planned to wander incognito today, to heighten my sense of adventure. Hauling out a 300mm zoom lens to capture book jackets and $200 library kits would be a sure way of blowing my cover. And I hadn't been kicked out of church since 1978, when somebody asked me what time it was during communion and I snuck a quick look at the Timex on my left wrist. Which was connected to my left hand, which was holding the grape juice that subsequently poured onto the crotch of my white jeans. (It was 1978. There were six other pairs of white jeans in the same pew.) I believe it was the poorly stifled laughter up and down the length of my pew that was the ultimate cause of the expulsion. Okay, no pictures today. I would simply observe.

I steadied my gaze on an eight-foot diameter table that stood between me and the coffee bar. I counted over twenty DVD titles, all professionally designed and packaged for retail. Titles like *Geology: A Biblical Viewpoint on the Age of The Earth (5 DVD set)*, *Does Biology Make Sense without Darwin?* and the *Ultimate Apologetics Box Set (4 DVDs)* let me know I'd arrived at the right church. After a ten-minute tour of the foyer, I dropped my lukewarm coffee into a trash bin and headed for the men's room. As I was standing at attention another gentlemen stepped up beside me and shouted out a hearty, "Good morning, brother!" These country folk sure were friendly.

I hastily exited the men's room and made my way into the auditorium, I scanned my surroundings and looked for a corner to hide in. It's not that I was nervous, but I planned on taking copious notes during the sermon and wouldn't want any stragglers from my home church to see this behavior and report back to my pastor. That would be awkward. I never take notes when he preaches.

I settled into the vacant balcony wing that descended from the rafters of the auditorium in a slender wedge down to the extreme right hand side of the platform. From my vantage point I would be able to see all the players in the worship band, and watch the faces of the entire congregation. As I took my seat, I noticed that across from me on the opposite balcony wing, a large contingent of people in brightly colored hoodies were finding their places. I later found out these Answers in Genesis evangelists would be trekking to Vancouver, where the Olympics were taking place, to hand out thousands of leaflets and spread the gospel to international tourists,

Irish House pub patrons and Danish speed skaters. These hoodie people had heard Ken Ham speak several times before and they were here for their pre-game speech.

I spotted several video cameras set up at different locations around the auditorium, but I didn't see any vacant microphone stands on the floor. With no question period on the agenda, I would have to either wait until the speaker was looking and shoot my hand up, or hide out in the parking lot until he packed up his DVDs. I pulled a notebook and pen from my bag. My digital recorder was blinking its readiness. I kept it hidden under my jacket to avoid trouble. I felt a slight rush of adrenaline, perhaps like what real reporters feel when they're about to get a scoop. *Ease up pal. You're not smuggling Bibles into North Korea.*

I was pulled from my secret agent visualization when a worship band of twenty somethings oozed onto the stage. I was struck with a puzzling thought. How do I worship wholeheartedly with these people, my fellow believers, when my sole intent for showing up this morning was to ambush the preacher? But as the first bars of a familiar song swelled, and the congregation stood and began clapping, I decided that my theological differences with the guest speaker didn't need to get in the way of my desire to worship. As I began belting out a familiar lyric, "God of Wonders beyond our galaxy..." Somewhere below me, in the congregation, a gentle lady in a floor length print dress and golden braid leaned over to her husband and whispered, "Don't look. Two-thirty. Who's that guy in the balcony? Yes, he's wearing blue jeans to church. He's the only one up there."

Nice cover.

Four songs, two announcements and one pastoral introduction later, Ken Ham approached the pulpit. He appeared from out of the audience like a fish migrating onto dry land. He engaged his polite audience with a couple of jokes about his Australian heritage, and an anecdote about the hardships he had to overcome in his journey all the way from Cincinnati, the home of his Creation Museum. I could sense immediately that he was comfortable in the pulpit, sure in his delivery, and familiar with his audience. He would be preaching to the choir today. He was passionate and methodical. Samuel Rowbotham, vibrant evangelist of the flat earth revival, would be proud. I hunkered down in my pew, like a pirate of the lowest rank assigned to the crows-nest, and reached for my pen.

Ken Ham preached for over an hour on the need for believers to take a stand against the secularization of schools and churches across Europe, America, Canada and Australia. The particular secularization he was referring to was, of course, the belief in a planet that was billions of years old, and inhabited by humans that had evolved from lower life forms over millions of years. He said that the battle line drawn between faith in Jesus and science is unavoidable, and that the victims are children. I agreed on the last point.

He talked about a survey conducted by a secular polling organization which asked specific questions to over one thousand college age kids who had walked away from the church. The statistics were depressing. According to the poll, two thirds of kids in our churches today are "Already Gone"—the title of Ham's recent book. He spoke about kids in grade school coming home with questions like "who made God anyway?" and "How did they fit all those animals on Noah's Ark?" and "What about the dinosaurs?" He preached that the reason that kids are abandoning their faith is because parents and Sunday school teachers have responded lamely with, "We don't know all the answers, but don't worry about it, Johnny. Just trust in Jesus."

The Answers in Genesis answer to all of this was that believers in Jesus needed to start teaching the scientific and historical truths of the first chapters of Genesis so that our kids will be able to defend their faith out there in the real world.

I was Already Gone.

I'm sure that his survey was properly conducted. I'm sure that they asked fair questions, and received honest answers. But I had some trouble with his analysis of the data, and the solution. I grew up in church, like the other adults in the survey. I attended Sunday school regularly, like the other adults in the survey. And I had to face serious doubts about my Christian faith just like the others in the survey. It didn't matter that it had taken me twenty-five years to entertain those doubts. Okay, I'm a slow doubter. When Ken Ham's sermon was over, he gave parents and grandparents the opportunity to come forward for prayer and repent of not teaching their children that God made the world six thousand years ago. I was distressed.

§

This collective crisis of faith is not going to be addressed by continuing to dole out the same answers that have resulted in hundreds of thousands of believers walking away from the faith of their parents at an early age. This crisis will only be averted when Christians stop hiding behind a brand of Bible literalism that is no more intrinsic to faith than a geocentric universe or a flat earth. Ham maintains that the hypocrisy of telling people to believe in Jesus and not worry about Genesis one to eleven is the source of our troubles. I still believe in Genesis chapter one to eleven, but I no longer feel the need to wring any biology or earth science from its pages.

I had an unshakeable faith in the God of the Bible. Ken Ham, meanwhile, standing not more than sixty feet away from me, was articulating in his affable Aussie accent a similar faith in the same God of the same Bible. And yet we were light years apart in our interpretation of the words that fill the pages of our common Scripture. How is it possible that two believers can be so connected via faith in Jesus Christ and yet so utterly divergent in the way they process the story?

Four hundred years ago, Galileo dared suggest that the solar system might be a little different than we had envisioned. Before Galileo we were ignorant. And God loved us. During the firestorm of criticism and debate that raged for almost a century after Galileo's cosmological assertions, God loved us. After a time we began to trust in our telescopes. We harnessed our divinely granted powers of reason to redraw the heavens and we realized that we'd been mistaken.

And God loved us.

Today, in small town Canada, I ponder my recent understanding of genetic modification and ice core samples and Hebrew poetic devices as I sat at the feet of a young earth creationist imploring a family of believers to hold fast to a simple about a six thousand year old earth and an ark big enough for two of every animal that ever existed, and room enough to spare for anyone else who dared believe.

And God loves us.

40

JUNK DNA

I t should be painfully obvious by now that I am not a scientist. Yet I am hounded by the temptation to flood these pages with incontrovertible evidence in support of evolutionary theory and a very old earth. I'd like to do that. It would be the heroic thing to do—the Hollywood way. Simply step up to the podium, pull out my laser pointer and connect the dots of biology and natural selection, radiometric dating and the fossil record, cosmological constants and the like, leaving my skeptics in teary-eyed conviction, full of remorse for their intellectual sins.

But it seems that even after spending six hours or more trying to master the intricacies of DNA, I'm not yet ready to hit the lecture circuit. I did, however, during my reading of *The Language of God* by Francis Collins, learn enough to get myself into trouble with every creationist on the block.

As Collins explains, the genetic information found in every cell in the human body has remarkable similarities to the DNA found in other living things. DNA, the genetic instruction book that enables a human body to repair itself and even make another human body, contains over three billion (that's three THOUSAND MILLION) lines of code. And much of that

DNA contains very long sequences of the same coding instructions as can be found in other living things. This is fact.

Every time a cell duplicates itself, an exact copy of the DNA instructions in the cell nucleus is also duplicated. Occasionally there are errors that occur during this procedure. It is these errors or mutations in the genetic code that actually change the nature of the cells that make up every living thing. What biologists now know (and what Darwin could only hint at) is that if the mutation has no negative affect on a creature's ability to survive, that mutation will essentially ride along in future generations, as non-functioning genetic inventory. They call it junk DNA.

Well, it's not really junk. It has a specific purpose, or did at one time, but no one knows what that is anymore. The name "Junk DNA" became the moniker of choice in the same way that the term SPAM came to represent those files in your inbox that seem totally unnecessary.

Let's continue with the computer analogy and see where this takes us.

Junk DNA is also very much like those files on your computer that you deleted last week. You don't need them. You don't want them. But unless you eradicate that unwanted data by intentionally returning your hard drive to its pristine factory settings, that unnecessary data will sit dormant on your computer collecting cyber dust. And as long as it doesn't get in the way of the useful stuff on your computer it will stay there forever. Just like junk DNA.

For example, as I've been writing this very book I've been careful to back-up the manuscript so I won't be tempted to launch myself off a freeway overpass should a lightning strike reduce my Macbook to a pile of glowing aluminum iGoo. Yesterday, I brought a new computer home to live with us. All of the data on my old iMac has now been transferred to the new one. The procedure, known as migration, allows all the files on my old computer to be transferred to the shiny new model. I now possess two machines that appear to be quite different on the outside but, as far as the data is concerned, are exact copies of each other.

Now, if I pick up my writing assignment where I left off before the migration, the new file on my new computer will begin to change over time. However, it won't be simply expanding from its original size. As I fix typos and revise entire paragraphs that were already in existence, the new file will evolve on several levels, diverging from the original back-up file that lies dormant on my old iMac.

Now let's leap forward six months, into an imaginary yet entirely plausible scenario.

In the future I am a wildly successful author, wealthy and famous perhaps, with an artificial tan and whiter teeth. I am also down one Mac due to a recent break-in.

One day I discover what looks like my old iMac, sitting in Sal's Pawn Shop ten blocks from my house. Sal the owner scoffs at my accusation of thievery, explaining that he bought it from a friend and it couldn't have been stolen. As I am not a proponent of vigilante justice and Sal, who outweighs me by at least sixty pounds and has an AK47 in the display case next to a fine selection of eighty-three karat gold pendants, I opt for caution. The wise thing would be to call the police so they can drive over and referee this dispute before one of us gets badly beaten and I go to the hospital.

But how would I prove to the police that the iMac at Sal's Pawnshop was originally mine? It would be quite simple, actually. First, I would call up my IT guru, my agnostic buddy Jack, and invite him over. I have no hesitation calling an agnostic to investigate, as his current theological disposition will have no negative bearing on his technological expertise.

The first thing Jack notices is that the desktop backgrounds are different, the passwords don't work, and the iTunes play-list doesn't resemble my musical taste in the slightest (I would never pay real money for a download of Hall and Oates). At first glance, my contention that Sal is trying to hawk my old iMac doesn't hold water. But then Jack assures me that unless the hard drive was intentionally wiped clean, there will be some old files, some of my previous work, sitting dormant on that old computer.

Sal is agitated, sensing that a valuable piece of inventory is about to be confiscated. He defends his position by suggesting that the rightful owner of this iMac, a big fan of Hall and Oates thank you very much, must have downloaded my book from the internet, thought it was crap and deleted it. His alibi, while personally hurtful, is a distinct possibility. How would I go about proving that Sal is lying?

My agnostic IT guru Jack explains to the officers that if we could recover even a few pages of my old manuscript from that hard drive and compare them with the same series of pages from a backed-up version of the manuscript that we migrated to my new iMac when I first bought it, we might have a chance.

"So what?" says Sal. "I already told you, my friend downloaded your stupid book. Hates your work. Hates it. Every word. Not believable. Uninspired. No Flow. Too many short sentences."

"But," I say bravely (praying that my lower lip doesn't begin its rarely called upon but highly effective scaredy-pants dance) "I'm not looking for the whole book. I'm looking for a piece of the same book—with mistakes!"

If after close inspection we discover that each pair of matching pages, one taken from each Mac, contained the identical mistakes, in the same location, paragraph after paragraph, we could draw only two conclusions. Either the old manuscript was accidentally copied to or from the old computer, or someone with access to both machines had inserted the same error-riddled data onto both hard drives. But in either case it would be the presence of errors that would link the two computers together. Spelling mistakes, improper punctuation and run-on sentences that occurred in the same position, page after page after page, would prove conclusively that one file was a replica of the other.

At this point in the story, Sal would hang his head in shame, the attending officers would ask for my autograph convinced that I was a direct descendent of Sherlock Holmes. I would cradle my precious old iMac lovingly in my arms and either head for the door or trade it in on a hedge trimmer.

§

DNA evidence for common ancestry between humans, chimpanzees, and other primates is even more compelling than the evidence in this example. I could spend a lot of effort telling similar stories trying to convince some people why evolution by natural selection is a true accounting of what actually happened. But I know better than that. As a Christian with a creationist past, I already know that hard scientific evidence is suspect, built on a foundation of false logic at best and hellish lies at worst. The creationist believes that God actually copied genetic mistakes into the DNA instruction manual of different species of primates, even though he created them *ex nihilo*—from nothing. If this was an oversight, I would respectfully suggest that the Intelligent Designer is less than God. If it happened on purpose, and some creationists suggest he did this to test our faith, then we have even bigger problems.

How might humans go about building trust with a deity that got his kicks out of playing those kind of games with creatures so limited in their ability to comprehend the evidence? The God that I want to know created man in his image, able to reason and discover the laws of nature. I am truly stuck if I start believing that my very God-given capacity for reason is the very thing that could separate me from finding him.

41

WHAT TO DO WITH GENESIS – TWO PRETTY GOOD IDEAS

"**W**hat if the evidence actually points to a long drawn-out period of time where humans evolved from lower life forms? And what if God was behind that process, allowing it to play through the eons before he breathed a soul into man?"

My brother didn't speak. I'd seen that look before. Never have figured out what that look means.

I continued.

"It can't be our ability to produce red blood cells, or convert sunlight into vitamin D that makes us like God. Whatever it is, it can't be our lung capacity, because God doesn't breathe oxygen. He invented the stuff. Isn't it our spirit that sets us apart from the mammals? Does it really have anything to do with our physical shell?"

"Why did God allow the text to say what it does?" said my brother.

"I know it sounds pretty simple in the English language version, but Hebrew scholars have been debating the literal meaning of Genesis since before Jesus was born. Doesn't that say something?"

"Genesis tells us that God created everything in six days," my brother replied.

"It does in English!" I responded.

"In every language!"

"How many do you speak?"

"None. Well one."

"How's your Hebrew?"

"Shut up!"

And so it went.

I kept up the debate with my brother, who at this moment was acting like a younger version of myself. It was as if I had stepped into that old life insurance commercial where a healthy young guy meets up with a silver-haired older version of himself. "How did we do?" asks the younger. "Not very well at all," says the older. "Once you started dabbling with Darwin you came off the rails. But we were hopeful and we prayed for you at Bible study every week."

"I didn't lose my faith?" says the younger.

"Not yet, but you will."

And I had.

But now I was back from the brink, dabbling with questions even more calamitous than my tricky escapade into evolutionary logic. My new challenge involved figuring out what to do with Genesis. If I was going to enjoy a comfortable deviation from a "literal" understanding of the first pages of the Bible I needed to come up with plan B.

I had heard the chatter about those creation "myths" from Bible skeptics, and I wasn't comfortable with that idea. The Greeks had their myths, but Zeus and Apollo didn't come pre-packaged with historical proofs, apart from archaeological evidence that these lesser gods were actually worshipped. Genesis, on the other hand, seemed at first read to be a continuous story where the curtain opened to the sights and sounds of God creating, and transitioned immediately into a twisting plot that included Adam, Abraham and Joseph and Moses and the Ten Commandments, and Israelites in the desert. And it seemed to be contained within a real-life geographical space, and along a seemingly compact timeline.

The trick now revolved around processing a creation account that had few, if any, ties to modern scientific thought, and at the same time upheld my conviction that the Old Testament, and Genesis in particular, could still be trusted as the inspired Word of God.

I soon discovered that I wasn't the only pilgrim on this road of theological discontent. While Richard Dawkins, Christopher Hitchens and their minions had been preaching to their own hymn-starved choirs about the inevitable crumbling of religion and how anyone who dared stand for a universe wrapped in a theistic framework would find themselves scorned into submission, there had been a growing wave of resistance against their polemic, fueled by thoughtful people of faith. The odd fact that these new ideas on biblical interpretation, flying under the radar of contemporary evangelicalism, had been energized by the same enlightenment fires that coaxed the new atheists out from under their rocks and into the public square only goes to prove that chasing the truth is never a vain pursuit.

Since the nineteenth century, geology—the study of the earth, and archaeology—the study of everything buried in it—had transformed what once were mild concerns about biblical interpretation into a full-fledged recalibration of everything we thought we knew about Old Testament history and ancient Middle Eastern culture. Again, the evangelical roots still tugging at my ankles were surely to blame for my ignorance on the matter, but showing up late to the party has always been my strong suit.

Three books (of many) that I've found helpful in processing what Genesis means and what it doesn't are: *The Lost World of Genesis One* by John H. Walton, *The Evolution of Adam* by Peter Enns, and *The Genesis Enigma* by Andrew Parker. The first two books table a new way of understanding Genesis based on recent revelations about the ancient world. The third book, by Parker, suggests that while Genesis chapter one is in no way a literal historical account, it may (against all odds which would make it a miracle from the mists of antiquity) be a scientifically accurate description by a pre-scientific observer of what actually happened in the beginning.

Pretty Good Idea #1

In both *The Lost World of Genesis One* and *The Evolution of Adam*, the authors make the case that the ancients never made a distinction between natural and supernatural as we do in the twenty-first century. People living in ancient times never really questioned who was behind the created order. Every culture had their own gods and mythologies to explain the natural world, and while there were competing ideas about which god had created what, the debate was never about whether or not a deity had been involved in the whole affair. In the ancient world, deities were constantly acting through material forces. Whether through rain, drought, fire, storms, birth defects or food poisoning, the gods were always busy, always at work behind the curtain.

The Hebrew account of creation differed from the stories of their Mesopotamian neighbors in that Genesis attributed creation of the entire cosmos to the handiwork of a single deity. While the creation myths of the Babylonians claimed the universe was the result of a violent struggle between the members of the cosmic ruling elite, complete with sword play and celestial love triangles (not to be confused with those groovy New Age Gordian knots) the Hebrew account stated emphatically that God— Yahweh—was responsible for all of it.

This was a revolutionary idea. In the ancient world, the lives of men were controlled by a ragtag assortment of impulsive gods and demigods, a hyper-dysfunctional strata council of sorts where alliances were sworn and swapped like promise rings at summer camp. And just like every other committee struck since the dawn of time, the results were pathetic.

In fact, no other ancient myths even hinted at a universe that could be tamed by a single God as the Hebrew storytellers claimed. And this Hebrew God didn't like to share the spotlight with anyone. The Sun God, for example, known as Ra to the Egyptians and Utu to the Babylonians, didn't even get a speaking part in Genesis. Not even a "thanks for coming out, we'll get back to you—enjoy this swell selection of parting gifts." The Hebrew God allowed—gave permission—to the greater light to rule the day, but that was it. The moon, itself a deity of dim repute even in pagan lore, was referred to simply as the lesser light. (Let's not get distracted with the literal meaning of the word light at this point. None of us are about to toss our current understanding of the moon as a reflector of light, in favour of the ancient Hebrew cosmological assertion that the moon was a producer of light. Yes, it's cherry picking, and we do it every time we read scripture.)

In the Hebrew version of creation, the oceans and seas—cradle of darkness, chaos and holding tank of evil, according to neighboring cultures—were not granted any innate powers to accomplish anything on their own. God alone divided the land from the seas and told the great mysterious deep to stay put. While Israel had indulged in multiple affairs with lesser deities during much of her history, there was only ONE god worth talking about and his name was Yahweh. He alone was in complete control of all the powerful forces of nature, both on the earth and above it.

In *The Lost World of Genesis One*, Walton further theorizes that the ancients understood creation as part of a process. The gods acted on earth when they wished to establish an earthly throne or court from which they could rule over mortals. The gods never made anything for its own sake. Creating was always tied to a purpose, like building furniture or spinning pottery. As a result of this worldview, the ancients didn't concern themselves with any in-depth analysis of the elements required or the chemistry invoked to bring a universe into being.

I mean, who needs the periodic table of elements when you can make everything you need out of earth, air, fire and water? (My chemistry teacher never did give in on this point, but I digress.) To the ancient mind, ultimate purpose was the underlying principle of any creative act. The earthly stage was simply a backdrop upon which the drama of the gods played out. The construction methods of such a universe were inconsequential. In the old world, only an idiot would think that the universe happened all by itself, and it would be at least thirty centuries before we had evolved enough of those to cause any real trouble.

The Hebrews understood the world to be quite a different place than what we now know it to be. The firmament, for example, which Genesis states divided the waters above from the waters below, was considered a barrier, a sort of crystalline tarp, which held all the water in the sky from falling to the ground. This makes sense when you live in a world that is flat, set on pillars to keep it steady. It would make sense to cover it with an enormous celestial sphere, like a snow globe, to keep the stars from crashing down on your camels. Life was simple. Most folks were trying to expand their working knowledge of masonry or bronze crafting. For thousands of years, raising vibrant yaks and trying to keep the grape juice from causing hallucinations was more important than proving the inverse square root of pi.

Peter Enns, while agreeing with Walton that we must carefully disassemble and then rebuild our expectations of Genesis, places his focus squarely on the comparative accounts of the neighboring empires as the contextual backdrop for the Hebrew creation accounts. Enns also draws from the extensive archaeological finds of the last two centuries to suggest that the Genesis story, drawing from both Hebrew antiquity as well as the history of their neighbors and captors, was the formal articulation of what Israel had believed all along, but kept forgetting. Assembled in final draft form only after the Babylonian exile, Genesis and in fact the entire Old Testament was intended to help the Jewish nation reconnect with their national identity as God's chosen people.

Enns is not the first Bible scholar to link the biblical creation and flood accounts with similar stories from other ancient civilizations. The Gilgamesh story, for example, recorded one thousand years before the Hebrew account, has striking parallels to Genesis and a flood account that are curious. This doesn't imply that my favorite Bible stories are fictional. What it does mean is they are rooted in real world thought, part of an age-old conversation between people groups and cultures. In fact, the ancient world doesn't seem quite so distant when I consider how present day conversations about God, justice and natural disaster are messed and muddled with popular notions of deity, and how people are supposed to live their lives and contemplate a God that we just can't make sense of.

Both Walton and Enns maintain that I needn't escape sanity and orthodoxy to entertain the thought of Genesis chapter one being something other than an attempt at science or journalistic history.

Pretty Good Idea #2

The third book in my recent trilogy of late night musings into alternative Genesis interpretation was a return to the scientific fodder of the creation-evolution debate. Andrew Parker became a household name, in microbiology households at least, with the publication of *In The Blink of An Eye* in 2003. Parker's light switch theory, which he detailed in that book, proposes that the evolutionary blast known as the Cambrian explosion, which occurred about 530 million years ago, was triggered by the introduction of sight into the chain of living beings (as in "Let there be light"). Parker's premise is that light sensitive cells, and the evolution of creatures with visual sensing abilities, led to the predator / prey relations that fuelled the development of the wide variety of life forms we see around us today. What Parker didn't foresee at the time his theory was published was its biblical implications. After getting an unusual number of requests from curious readers, Parker did further study, with a Bible beside his biology notebooks, and became convinced that Genesis chapter one, while not a true chronological account (ignore the six days) did lay out a scientifically accurate telling of the formation of our planet.

He started by relating the Big Bang with verse one: "In the beginning God created the heavens and the earth." So far this doesn't sound like too much of a stretch for either a scientist or a Bible believer. However, as Parker investigated the verses that followed, he became convinced that something spectacular had taken place in the formation of the biblical account.

For example, the gathering of the seas in Genesis 1:6-10 includes no scientific explanation of how H_2O appeared on our planet, only that Yahweh said "Let there be" or "Let it happen." As has already been mentioned, according to ancient cultural norms, the Genesis author would have every reason to believe that the oceans were the source of darkness and evil, invested themselves with godlike powers. To suggest that the waters became divided from the land at God's command was both revolutionary and an exact telling of what happened. The ancients had no conceptual basis for a planet that had cooled down over time to the point where oxygen and hydrogen atoms escaping into the freshly forming atmosphere could reconfigure as H_2O and fall back to the surface where they collected in the depressed regions of the earths crust as it continued its tectonic waltz that we recognize today as continental drift.

It was in these primordial seas that Parker's light switch theory takes the stage. At the command of God, the planet begins to "bring forth grass" in verse eleven. The words grass or vegetation, visible to the naked eye of both ancient authors and ancient readers, was the only vocabulary at their disposal to describe what appeared on earth after the seas had been formed. Without having access to any modern scientific understanding of the first life forms—the single-celled photosynthesizing organisms that started the chain of life in the oceans—the Genesis account gets it right.

In verse twenty of Genesis chapter one, by the time the atmosphere was fully formed and the greater and lesser lights were now visible, God commands the oceans to teem with life. Parker, a twenty-first century evolutionary biologist with scant prior interest in the biblical account, was hooked. In his estimation, Yahweh's next instructions, which called for the introduction of whales, then land mammals and finally birds BEFORE any living creatures appeared on land, were more than coincidence. Parker's conclusion that the accepted progression in evolutionary theory lines up perfectly with the biblical record caused him to make the following assertion: "The opening page of Genesis is scientifically accurate, but was written long before the science was known... I have never before encountered such powerful, impartial evidence to suggest that the Bible is the product of divine inspiration."

Parker contends that while a recent six-day creation is laughable, a metaphorical reading of Genesis is powerful evidence in favor of an inspired source for Genesis. He suggests that Moses, the desert dweller, raised in the polytheistic courts of Egypt, would have no human way of laying out the creation events in the correct scientific order unless he had been given insight into those events by God directly.

§

It is tempting to hitch my wagon to one of these aforementioned perspectives, but if I've learned anything in my journey it is this: don't. Don't jump too soon. Don't fall for frail certainty when mystery is even more satisfying. Don't ever post a warning on the church door that includes more than these words: WET PAINT! Does this mean I am merely trying to avoid the unpleasant consequences of siding with an unpopular theological position? Probably. It may also mean that I am finally learning that reason is not the opposite of faith, but a valuable complement to it.

My life-long faith in the Bible, which had only recently been reduced to rubble in the asking of a few simple questions, is showing definite signs of life. It is starting to resemble something solid again. That sound underfoot isn't the sucking sound of quicksand. It's bedrock. Kick at it. Stomp on it. Stand on it.

42

AFTER ITS KIND

As a lifelong member of the evangelical community, I know that nothing gets a pod of creationists, young-earthers and old-earthers alike, more agitated than when somebody suggests that "variation over long periods of time" is the mechanism that drives evolution forward. This particular hot button has at least two live wires connecting it to something incendiary.

First, there is the commonly held understanding that humans haven't been around long enough to witness evolution so it couldn't have happened. But that's why it's called scientific inquiry and not show and tell. Just as in murder, the evidence gathered at the scene of a genetic crime can be compelling and conclusive if pieced together properly.

The second flash point that creationists gravitate toward is the apparent obvious command in Genesis where God tells all living things to reproduce 'after their kind.' (The fact that our English translations say that God instructed the waters to "swarm" or "teem" with life and the earth itself to "bring forth" are hints at some sort of natural process. The Hebrew writers, even in their inspired state, didn't rely on the word 'create' to describe what God initiated at this point in the story. Hopefully, this tiny grammatical deviation away from any notion of instant creation is troubling for all those *ex nihilo* fans in the audience.)

'After its kind' is the rallying cry of the anti-evolutionist who has no room for natural selection to act beyond the borders of species. While micro-evolution, the notion that change within species is acceptable (and scientifically proven and acknowledged by creationists), macro evolution, the idea that an animal can actually morph into another type of animal altogether, seems far fetched, counterintuitive and more importantly, anti-biblical. So, in keeping with my penchant for stirring the primordial pot, let's take a closer look.

If we were to go out to an auto graveyard, on the edge of town, we'd discover dozens of cars that look like they were "descended" from one another. If we decided to get our hands dirty, and dismantle any of these relics, we'd unearth distributor caps, spark plugs, steering columns, hundreds of related parts that always seemed to show up in roughly the same place no matter which car we searched.

However with all those car parts to sift through, would we ever think for a moment that a headlight on a Mercury Comet had evolved from the headlight on a Dodge Duster? Never. We would agree that it was obviously a designed part, and that any successful design innovation in one car doesn't appear miraculously in another vehicle. The designers back at the factory, happy with a feature, had worked it into next year's model. The point being, all of the so-called evolving was actually done by a designer, or, more likely, whole teams of designers. Each designer wasn't physically dragging parts from a previous model to build next year's new and improved. They were simply starting from scratch – *ex nihilo* – back at the drawing *board* and building upon earlier design successes.

To a young earth creationist, who can't allow for millions of years of change, the auto graveyard is very similar to what we find in nature. God simply created creatures quite like ones He'd already made because He saw that his work was good. He made slight design changes, but built from the ground up. However, while the natural world with its two million living species (and millions more surviving only in the fossil record) might be very much like a used car lot, give or take a few fender benders, after close inspection the car analogy gets left up on blocks.

In his book *The Greatest Show on Earth*, biologist (and avid atheist) Richard Dawkins states that zoological terms like species, genera and phyla are completely human constructs invented solely for the purpose of allowing us to sort and categorize the mountains of species data available to us. Dawkins suggests that a species doesn't represent the way nature actually is—only the way we've been able to organize it.

It is common for paleontologists to disagree on the proper classification of a particular fossil, and often the original classification changes over time, as new data comes to the surface. Dawkins contends that if we possessed a fossil representing every stage of development of life on earth we would be in quite a predicament, because we'd have no missing links. And no missing links would leave us unable to delineate between one species and the next, simply because every child looks almost exactly like their parents. In Dawkins' world, the 'missing link' that the creationists keep ranting about is a great blessing. Missing links are those gaps in the fossil record that have made it possible for us to categorize species at all. There has never been a point in our planet's history when parents looked with horrified faces at their newly born offspring and said, "He's not ours!" That doesn't happen until puberty.

This thing called macro-evolution is not simply the unsupported contention of a weekend bug collector, suggesting that one species becomes another species entirely when an asteroid the size of Manhattan messes up the Yucatan peninsula, or a frog accidently gets cuddly with a newt. No, macro-evolution, or as the biologist community likes to call it, history, is a highly detailed explanation of how microscopic change—a change that confers a reproductive advantage—has resulted in the vast variation of species we see in nature.

For example, if a mutation, a copying error in the DNA that gives instructions for the proteins that build muscle tissues, enables a gazelle to outrun the other gazelles, he will be more likely to escape a predator. His successful scamper across the savannah will not only keep him alive another day, it will also increase his chances of finding a mate. Studies have shown that uber-athletic gazelles attract females at an even higher rate than the well documented "quarterback-cheerleader magnet coefficient" as witnessed in colleges across the land.

However, history has also shown that our prize gazelle's high level of fitness means trouble for his neighbor, the all too common "kick sand in my face" gazelle. This unfortunate creature struggles along with white tape on his glasses and a pre-existing condition, which results in slower firing of the muscles fibers of his scrawny legs. However, while being less physically gifted makes gazelle number two a huge risk for the insurance companies and long shot to make the cover of National Geographic without some serious airbrushing, he is nonetheless a tasty and nutritious specimen, sure to help any famished cheetah reach his or her feline potential. In this case, as cruel as it sounds, we should be happy that the genetic dice that rolled out a slightly slower and hopelessly nearsighted gazelle were never passed on to future generations. Darwin had a name for this painful balance within nature. He called it natural selection.

However, while our faster gazelle was able to outrun most of his troubles he wasn't entirely spared of genetic variation. He also has some mutations in his DNA, but they didn't affect his ability to reproduce. Some mutations, as it turns out, are neither positive nor negative. So rather than being culled from the gazelle population, they are passed from parent to offspring. They simply go along for the genetic ride. After several generations or several dozen generations and a branch or two on the evolutionary tree, we should still be able to find that non–threatening mutation in the genetic code of our gazelle's great-great grandchildren, but many of them wouldn't be gazelles anymore. They would be impalas or springboks, cousins on the evolutionary tree of life. Somewhere along the family line, our gazelle's offspring had become separated into groups, through herd grazing patterns, or some other form of geographical isolation. Over time, their genetic variations allowed them to drift further and further from the characteristics that made them all look and perform like their famous Uncle Buck.

Let's wander back to the auto-wreckers for a moment. While my argument for design in the car analogy held up when it concerned innovation—or positive mutation—my theory (which is analogous to the intelligent design argument) breaks down miserably once we start examining deficiencies or mistakes in the design of each car.

For example, if two cars, both with a history of braking problems, were examined side by side, it might be possible to prove that a mechanical weakness in Model A had originated in Model B. If the faulty part in the brake line was manufactured by the same third party vendor, and sold to both car companies, which would be quite easy to confirm by checking the engineering records and parts inventory invoices (auto DNA) locked up at the plant, we would have indeed found a common design fault in two different cars—a genetic mutation. We would have proved bad design, and left a highly esteemed automotive brake manufacturer with a hefty legal bill.

§

Today we see evidence of what the creationists call microevolution—change within species—happening all through nature according to well documented laws of natural selection. This is exactly what we would expect to find. Consider this: Every living creature in the history of planet earth has been the child of a parent, identical in almost every respect, with only the tiniest of variation. Some of those variations presented the offspring with a competitive advantage in the wild (at the expense of others). Some of these variations had no effect on the creatures' ability to live a full and reproductive life.

Thus, when we read in Genesis that God commanded the animals to bring forth life "after their own kind," He was simply suggesting that they do exactly what biologists claim has been happening all along. God's directive to his creation was that it unfold, play the game, according to the seemingly unguided laws (only recently discovered by Mr. Darwin) of natural selection. The biblical phrase "according to its kind" does not preclude evolutionary patterns from emerging over time any more than it precludes God from upholding creation by his very hand at every turn in the struggle for biological life. Evolution doesn't have the authority to force God out of the picture because evolutionary theory is only capable of explaining the 'how' and was never intended to explain the 'why'. Why is a question for the theologians and philosophers. As a believer in an Ultimate Cause, a personal intelligence behind everything I see in nature, I am no longer threatened by the demands of the skeptic that God, if he exists at all, be relegated to the conceptual fringes of his creation, as if leaving the deist's God out of the equation somehow implies his obsolescence.

So while the Intelligent Design camp might be waving the flag of microevolution as an olive branch to the scientific community to indicate their willingness to meet halfway in the animal kingdom, there isn't a halfway point. There is no line in the sand between the 'micro'—change within a species, and the "macro"—divergence from common ancestors based on a creature's ability to adapt in the wild. The micro/macro argument, as it turns out, is a construct of the creationists.

43

BUT I DON'T WANT TO BE A CREATIONIST ANYMORE

Sometimes they call themselves Christ followers. In TV interviews, sociologist and speaker Tony Campolo speaks of "red letter" Christians. He is referring to the text in some printings of the Bible that is printed in red ink to delineate the actual words of Jesus. It seems like a lot of Christians these days don't want to get mistaken for, well, Christians. The obvious question is why a person who believes that Jesus is the Messiah, God's son, wouldn't want to be categorized as Christian. While the answer to many believers who have witnessed the recent besmirching of our demographic seems obvious, a better question is why someone would choose to taint their reputation with a quasi-political grouping that is routinely demonized in the media and on the street corner as intolerant, ignorant, judgmental, racist, bigoted, imperialistic, hypocritical and generally joyless. Not exactly the attributes that come to mind whenever we think of Jesus.

While I'm not quite ready to make that call to the census bureau and demand they dig up my form, scratch out my current religious affiliation and replace it with something more appropriate (like Fisherman's friend) I wonder if our community of faith has squeezed all the mileage it can out of the term Christian. I also find myself in a similar predicament with that other word I've often used to describe my scientific worldview. And I don't have any hesitation when I say, "I don't want to be a creationist anymore." The culture I've grown up in has unwittingly ruined that moniker for people like me who believe that we are on this planet for a purpose, but didn't arrive in one piece a few thousand years ago. But, on the other hand, I don't want to call myself an evolutionist because that makes me appear way too fatalistic.

Somebody asked me if I was into theistic evolution. "No," I said. "Not anymore than I am into theistic meteorology, or theistic dermatology or theistic gravitational theory." Bottom line—everything about the world that I live in is seen through the lens of theology. So let's just cut to the chase. Evolution leads straight back to a creator anyway if we are consistent with the boundaries of science, but because the rhetoric emanating from both sides of this debate has propped up a decades-old notion that evolution is anti-God, I need to find a better handle. The term Darwinist doesn't fair much better. So what am I?

In his book, *The Language of God*, Francis Collins uses the word Bio-Logos, an impressive term that implies both acceptance of the Natural Sciences and divine cause. I'm okay with Bio-Logos, but it doesn't have quite the ring I was hoping for.

Suppose I'm standing in line at Starbucks and the guy ahead of me in line says, "Hey, nice glasses, and I don't mean to pry, but are you an evolutionist or creationist?" To which I would proudly reply, "No, I'm a Bio-Logosolite." And then the next morning when I return to Starbucks for my meds and the barista says, " Hey, aren't you one of those Bio-Logosians?" I would reply, "I'm sorry you're mistaken. The Bio-Logosians were annihilated when they strayed into Kardasian air space." No, Bio-Logos definitely won't cut it. Love the website. Not sold on the name.

What if I were Creavolutionary? Or a Devolutionist with a capital D signifying my belief in a divine agent? Do I need to put myself in either camp? What was Jesus? He didn't mind being called Rabbi, so perhaps I'm being a little sensitive, but this newly found place of solid ground that I find myself staking claim to needs a name. And Newfoundland is already spoken for. It's impossible to print up T-shirts and hawk bumper stickers without a great name. And getting tax-free status involves so much paperwork that I have to get it right the first time. This naming exercise should be easy for me, as I'm a designer at heart. Branding is all about selling what you're selling in seven seconds or less. Let's see, how about... Okay, I've come to a decision. Send up the white smoke!

My journey onto the slippery slope has convinced me of the Grand Unified Purposes and Processes of Yahweh—or GUPPY for short. Like all brilliant acronyms, it's both memorable and screams for inclusion in the next best seller by Dan Brown. And catchy is only the beginning. It has that certain "oceans-teeming-with life" flavor that we read about in Genesis and still tips its hat in homage to those gill slits I enjoyed as an embryo while my mom was fighting off morning sickness.

I suppose if I'm going to follow convention, however, I should spell it in Greek, stamp it in chrome and glue it to all the sedans in our church parking lot next Sunday. Here it is in the original Greek (gamma upsilon pi pi psi) and it appears even more staggering in its simplicity and depth.

The twin pi's represent the two spheres of thought, religious and scientific. This may truly be the best of both worlds. If GUPPY holds up to the vetting process of both my old Sunday school teacher and the editors at *Scientific American* I will have successfully repurposed the sign of the early

Christians and reintroduced it in a way that appeals to anyone intent on holding tight to both their Bible and their biology textbook.

ENTER THE GUPPY
GRAND UNIFIED PURPOSES AND PROCESSES OF YAHWEH

GAMMA UPSILON PI PI UPSILON

"But why?" you ask. "Why don't you want to be a creationist anymore?"

Well, now that the genetically modified cat is out of the bag, so to speak, and my newly acquired affinity for Darwin's idea of natural selection is obvious, I feel I should take the time to say a few words to any creationist sympathizers who have not yet repurposed this book as fuel for the backyard fire pit.

It is one thing to defend one's position on a matter as long as the evidence can be debated and evaluated in an objective manner. However, there comes a time in every argument when a decision must be rendered and life moves on. For the Bible scientists, that time has come. Regardless of whether you believe that Scripture is inspired by God and speaks into the lives of twenty-first century problems, or is simply a collection of dusty writings collated to preserve the stories and customs of the ancient

Hebrews, there is one question that must be faced squarely: What is Bible science good for?

Well, not counting the cottage industry which has grown up around the debate and includes everything from DVD series to coloring books and family camps to second rate amusement parks and quirky museums, the correct answer is absolutely nothing.

Bible science doesn't actually do anything. Bible science, creationism, for all of its inspirational overtones and claims of upholding ultimate truth, has yet to submit a single invention to the US patent office. Bible science, in its adherence to Genesis as the pinnacle of geological, biological, anthropological, zoological and cosmological authority, has never successfully presented a theory of anything that has held up to the rigors of your plain old everyday "get out your microscope" brand of science. Ever.

Claiming to be a scientifically valid theory capable of answering the really deep questions of life, Bible science fails to answer even the simplest ones. Those in the creationism corner cannot hold up a single example of a testable Bible science prediction that, according to their theory of how things work, actually works. Parading an alternate theory of how the Grand Canyon formed in three weeks during Noah's flood is one thing. However, using that theory to lock up millions of investment dollars to drill for natural gas is quite another. Real science solves real world problems. Bible science so far hasn't solved a single one.

"But Bible science is an historical science. It doesn't make predictions about the future." That is correct. Evolution is also an historical science. And evolutionary scientists make predictions all the time about where (in the future) on the planet certain fossils can be located and at which strata in the geologic record certain life forms will be discovered.

Bible science as a discipline is unable, using flood geology and its ultra-short timeline, to make any testable predictions about speciation and diversity of life forms across the planet. Bible scientists working with both the knowledge of Noah's ark, which settled somewhere in the Turkish back country, and a well-documented marsupial Mecca in Australia, have not yet been able to come up with any theory to uncover migration patterns in the fossil record to help tell the story of how a tiny population (perhaps a dozen) of kangaroos, koalas, wallabies, platypuses, wombats, etc. managed to travel from the mountains of Ararat to the land down under without leaving a single trace of their journey (no dead uncles) and in the case of the koala bear, with no access to the only food (eucalyptus) that they must have in order to survive.

Real world bio-geographers, on the other hand, have been able to predict with certainty where the fossil remains of the nearest ancestors to the marsupials (an evolutionary idea) would be located. They did this after researching fossil finds on the west coast of Africa, as well as similar finds on the eastern shores of South America, and integrated those discoveries with general knowledge of comparative anatomy and geological understanding of plate tectonics. And they backed up their theory by renting a really big boat loaded up with hot chocolate and long underwear, and by traveling all the way to the Antarctic, where they set up dig sites and located the fossil intermediaries which link Australia's mammal population to their nearest cousins, extinct but well preserved, on neighboring continents. Real science solves real puzzles.

44

RESURRECTION THEORY

I am reading a book about creationism. Not sure why I decided to pick one up now, but you never know when a new idea might burst on the scene. A friend handed me this book hoping it would help me. Lend a little perspective. The author spends most of the book explaining why people who believe in evolution aren't really Bible believers. He has ninety-nine reasons why the Genesis story and evolution can't co-exist.

This author (who shall remain unnamed) claims that the scientific evidence actually points to a very young earth as seen in all the evidence of Noah's global flood. Continental drift, for example, is a myth because you can't drag the continents anywhere (they would break) and the Big Bang isn't a biblical concept because earth was created on day one, and the sun and stars not until day four. (How did you separate the first three days of creation without any sunlight? Oh never mind.) He also maintains that dinosaurs were taken aboard the ark, and wandered off after the flood, spawning all those medieval dragon stories. Those are four of his ideas. There are ninety-five more, and every chapter starts with a scripture verse. I think this was done on purpose to impress the reader and add a sense of gravitas to every other word on the page.

I am reminded as I read that the author is a Protestant. Turns out, there aren't any creationism books written by Catholics. None. Catholics don't have any problem with evolution as long as the science dictates a distinct mechanism for physical bodies, separate from the creation of souls, which are a special creation of God. In a letter from Pope Pius XII, dated August 1950, the Catholic Church outlined its understanding of evolution. And then in 1996, Pope John Paul II clarified the position.

A vast majority of evangelical Protestants, on the other hand, see things differently. As a "protesting" Christian you're allowed to read the Bible for yourself—at least that was the original claim to fame of the reformers. Reading the Bible and adult baptism were two biggies. But mostly reading the Bible for yourself. God talks to you directly, and you get to talk back without waiting in line for a priest to translate. It's part of what makes Protestants proud. And frustrating. Because while you're allowed to interpret the Bible for yourself, you have be careful that you don't upset other people by disagreeing with their own interpretation. It's a crazy little dance we Protestants do which is oddly ironic since all the evidence I've seen would suggest that Catholics are much better dancers.

§

I had the phone to my ear taking notes. My dad had been telling me all about Resurrection Theory when we got sidetracked.

"Well, I'm reading a book on creationism. First one I've read in a long time," I said. "There's not much to their global flood theories, and the young earth stuff. But you have to give the Bible science guys some credit for putting so much weight on the doctrine of original sin. They are quite convinced that Adam's disobedience in the garden was the trigger point for all the natural evil in the world."

"Explain that again," said my dad. I have to remind myself to slow down. Dad's been a little under the weather for several months now. The chemotherapy is almost over, and whatever it was that attacked the healthy cells in his body was cornered and evicted months ago. At least that's what the doctors have told us. During his recovery, my dad has been working through the thorny little theological problem of pain and suffering in a world created by a good God. Cancer patients have this uncanny ability to scrape off the whip cream and dig into the Jell-O. One day when I was driving him to the cancer clinic, I brought up that verse in the New Testament where Jesus says that unless a kernel of wheat falls into the ground and dies there can't be any new life. I did not say this to cheer him up.

I'd like to think my dad took that as license to begin building an entire doctoral thesis on Resurrection Theory—the idea that all of Scripture, beginning with Adam, and running through the Exodus, to Jesus and finally the writing of the Apostle Paul—are presenting the case that in God's created order, death always precedes life. It's the only way anything works in our corner of the universe.

"Well, here's the lynchpin of their argument, and it's the only piece of the puzzle that has any teeth to it," I said mixing my metaphors recklessly. "Death is the result of sin. Adam sinned when he and Eve ate from the tree of the knowledge of good and evil. Therefore death did not exist before Adam committed the transgression. Because death wasn't active, there were no carnivorous animals, or predatory patterns in the animal kingdom, or extinction of species. According to creationists, God's warning to Adam that disobedience would result in death is scriptural proof that death didn't exist in any form prior to the fall."

"But Adam didn't die after he sinned," said my dad. "Not physically, anyway. So that reference to death doesn't mesh with what the author is attempting to prove. If Adam had physically died, dropped dead in the garden from fruit poisoning, you could make the case. But after being evicted from Eden, Adam and Eve were forced into a place of thorns and blood and sweat, outside the protection of the garden. Adam had kids, a blue collar career in agriculture, and died an old man."

"Tell me more about Resurrection theory," I asked him. "Have you made any progress or sketched your ideas into a framework?"

"Well, all these discussions we've been having about your journey, they are part of a larger issue. I keep running into people at the coffee shop or over at the cancer clinic who are eager to talk about God. But many people who've grown up in a church context have questions. And a lot of them are simply turning away, shaking their heads, saying, "I can't live in that world any longer."

"Which world are you talking about?" I asked.

"That world that your creationist author lives in. After a certain point people grow weary of trying to make that young earth interpretation of the

Bible fit with the science that we operate in everyday. Eventually, people give up believing that the two opposing views can be reconciled, so they pack up their spirituality and go for a burger. It's a lot less work."

"So is this resurrection theory you're working through about integrating the two?"

"Just like you're doing, except it's been a lot easier for you because for you theology is a hobby. For me it's been a career, and it takes longer to turn this ship around. You have to remember, I've been preaching some of this stuff for fifty years."

He's right. I can change my mind without inflicting too much collateral damage. But when you're a shepherd you can't run around willy-nilly rethinking your theology out loud. It unnerves the sheep. People depend on you. For a preacher, unwavering doctrinal consistency ranks right up there with love of early-morning prayer and mandatory table grace even if you're only eating pie.

"Has Mom stepped away from the ledge?" I asked him, referring to her concern for my Darwin dabbling.

"I don't think she's too far behind on this. Your mom claims you never got your young earth ideas from us. But you had her worried for a while. She thinks you're obsessing."

"Can you repeat that?" I was peeling a banana from the bottom. "Did you know chimps peel bananas from the bottom? I wonder why we switched?"

He didn't bite.

"Do you think when you're done with your book, you'll be able to go back?" asked my dad.

I put down the top half of the banana.

"Go back? You mean recalibrate my watch to a ten-thousand-year-old universe? No chance. And for the record, I never planned on ending up here. I am as shocked about this turn as you are."

"So, you don't see any middle ground?"

"I'm totally ready to change my mind, if that's what you're asking, but it will only happen if the scientific community make some adjustments based on new evidence. But you're right about the middle ground. I doubt I'll ever be able to convince a dyed-in-the-wool creationist that evolution fits within a biblical worldview; I'm going to have to come to terms with that."

"You can't get too worked up trying to make people believe something they have no intention of believing. Just keep talking. Keep telling your story," said my dad. "That's all you can do."

45

CIRCUS

"**Y**ou're going where?" said Cory, my pastor friend, when I told him of my plans to go listen to a creationist speaker. His eyes grew wide, and his cheeks scrunched up, almost hidden behind his glasses. I could tell by the facial contortions that our ongoing discussions on Genesis had been an unqualified success.

"I'm sort of forcing myself to go," I replied. "I don't want to become so angry that I end up harboring the same level of disdain for creationists that I used to reserve for evolutionists. I'm really trying to be an equal opportunity disdainer. And besides, what could anyone say at this point that would change my mind? Maybe that's why I'm making myself go."

After all this researching and reading and finding new ways of angering my conservative friends, even entertaining the thought that a creationist could add something relevant to my new take on the universe is weirding me out. If this guy gets up to the podium and starts making sense, I will have a breakdown. Right there, in the tidy, pleasant confines of the auditorium at a nearby Christian school—I'll lose it. I can see the headlines now: "Evolutionist tasered after running amok at young earth rally."

According to the full-color poster attached to the email (the one which I'm supposed to put up at my local church, that accidentally got made into a cootie catcher) the lecture to be delivered by Jonathan Sarfati, from New Zealand, was being promoted as "The Greatest Hoax on Earth." Sarfati's presentation will be a detailed response to Richard Dawkins' latest book, *The Greatest Show on Earth: Evidence for Evolution*. I loved that book. I expect this evening will be awkward, but I promised myself that if I sat politely, tried to blend in with the other attendees, and that if I was patient, I might hear something profound, a solitary shred of evidence to entice me back over the fence, onto the side with the greener, fresher, ten-thousand-year-old grass.

Not accustomed to playing the part of introverted-brooding-skeptic-with-an-agenda, I debated whether I should keep my head down and try to fit in with this crowd or make a bold statement and voice my opposition to the inevitable Darwin bashing. Dropping a ten spot into the collection bucket would be a sign of good faith (New Zealand is a long way from everywhere) if I wanted to make friends tonight, but when the bucket passed by I was tempted to take out a twenty. *Anything to keep these people from doing more damage.* If only I'd printed up some of those WWDW?—What Would Darwin Do?—t-shirts. That would have been a perfect wardrobe choice. I should have ordered a few in New Mexico Red to mask the results of an impromptu bloodletting.

Perhaps striking up a friendly conversation with the creationist sympathizer in the next row would make for a more productive evening. Would it be okay to admit my change of heart, my treason, on this issue? Okay, so perhaps I'm wound up a little tighter than I thought, but I've invested too much in this to turncoat now. If I can just focus on all the reasons why creationism can't be true, I'll be okay. I think it's called whistling in the dark.

Atheism and evolution—I lost track of how many times I heard the speaker link those two concepts that evening. To a creationist, the dogma of the former is contingent on the conviction of the latter. At first I had expected to be taken aback with some new twists on the Intelligent Design arguments. However, as the evening wore on, I realized there weren't any new wrinkles in the plot. I did hear again that one-third of churched young people plan to leave their faith behind when they hit college, and that we should do something about that. I agree. But apart from a curious aside about carbon-14, which has a half life of approximately 5,700 years, being discovered in diamonds which are supposedly one hundred million years old (unexpected homework) I heard nothing to challenge my now solid conviction that Intelligent Design isn't very intelligent, and godless evolution is anything but godless.

I'm sure Sarfati's heart was in it, but being witness to such wasted theological effort was simply agonizing. Like watching a baptism in a sandbox.

I was tempted to crawl over the three pastors on my left, into the aisle, step up to microphone number two and ask the speaker why he felt the need to imply that atheism and evolution were inextricably linked. I was, after all, living proof that a person can believe in both the Bible AND evolutionary biology. To an audience heavily weighted on the side of creationism, I would surely have been a real live missing link, if I'd been willing to come out of my theological closet and make a public defense of my new found faith in faith AND science. But at that moment, in that auditorium, I might have been safer telling people I was gay.

At one point in the Q&A, a courageous physics major stepped up to the microphone and politely asked why Christians were so opposed to real science. After three uneasy minutes at the microphone she simply sighed. She thanked the speaker for listening to her concerns and turned in the direction of the exit doors.

Filled with an unfamiliar confidence and passion, I bolted out of my chair, and made my escape from the confines of the auditorium. I dashed about in the lobby before racing out the doors into the night in search of the searcher. I caught up to her. I thanked her for having the courage to stand and ask her questions. I encouraged her to keep investigating. I told her that the message of Jesus didn't conflict with anything she already knew about physics or biology. She seemed genuinely pleased at my attempt to make amends.

I took the opportunity to pass along a couple of authors I knew would be helpful, and I told her that the supposed proclamation of faith she had just witnessed was not orthodoxy. I think I used the word "circus" to describe the proceedings. We parted and I marched back indoors, energized by my recklessness.

As I made my way back inside the auditorium, I couldn't help wondering if I'd been over-the-top with my circus analogy? Perhaps not. A real circus comes with a marching band and a train of elephants followed by clowns with shovels. This event was lacking both the marching band and the elephants.

I had surprised myself with the brute boldness that had compelled me to engage in a faith conversation with a complete stranger. Bravado and optimism in the face of doubt and skepticism hasn't exactly been my hallmark in times past. I think I'm looking forward to my next conversation with my agnostic friend Jack.

46

AMAZING GRACE

"Amazing Grace how sweet the sound
that saved a wretch like me
I once was lost but now am found
was blind but now I see"

"Amazing Grace" is possibly the most well-known song in the English language. This old hymn, penned in 1779 by John Newton, a reformed slave trader, has become the rallying cry of several generations of God seekers around the world. It has reached such lofty heights due to the fact that it is an inspired piece of art. According to songwriters' lore, there is a time and space, or something sort of like time and space, where songs reside before they arrive on planet earth to be translated into music and language by a human author.

Being a musician, I have some understanding of the mystical nature of songwriting, and I think it would be beneficial to explain why I believe "Amazing Grace" is such a powerful song. But what does an old hymn have to do with the war between science and faith, you ask? Well, if you'll just follow along, my point will become clear shortly.

I'll use the first verse for our example. The first line, *"Amazing Grace how sweet the sound"* contains six words, a combination of two nouns, two corresponding adjectives, a definite article and adverb acting as an intensifier. The second line also contains six words: *"That saved a wretch like me."* Line three: *"I once was lost but now am found"* contains eight words, and line four *"was blind but now I see"* again has six. I know we're only scratching the surface, but stick with me.

If we dig deeper into what makes "Amazing Grace" so amazing, we quickly discover that each of those six words in the first line of the song contain a precise series of eleven vowels and seventeen consonants. The first word, "Amazing," contains a short 'a' as well as a long 'a'. The second word, "Grace," begins masterfully with a hard 'g,' and incorporates a short 'a,' a soft 'c' and finishes with an understated silent 'e.' Jumping to the last word of line one we discover a tricky little diphthong—the word "sound" (which is also a noun in this case) is pronounced with a sustained vowel 'ah,' formed by the tongue, followed immediately with a shorter second vowel 'oo' sound formed with the lips.

The first four lines of this hymn are assembled in the classic ABAB rhyming scheme similar to a Shakespearean sonnet. In this type of rhyme scheme, the last word in both the first and third lines have similar ending sounds while the last word in lines two and four also have end rhymes, but these rhymes are distinctly different than the offsetting pair.

Sound. Found.
Me. See.

Rhyming adds a predictable pattern to any lyric, making it easy to remember. The first couplet (two lines) includes alliteration, which is the use of the same consonant sound at the beginning of at least two closely aligned words— "sweet" and "sound" and "saved." I'm sure you'll agree that it is brilliant nuances such as this that have surely helped "Amazing Grace" become an icon in music history. But there's so much more. How often do we simply recite the lines of this or any song devoid of any musical backdrop? Hardly ever! As a musician, I can tell you that it is the music framing the composition that really begins to unveil the genius of the writer.

For starters, this tune, written in 3/4 time, is a waltz even though I doubt you'll ever see anyone using it as the first dance at their wedding reception. Its simple 1-2-3, 1-2-3 rhythm is a latticework upon which we string the syllables of each line like patio lanterns. In our example, the first lyrical sound—the 'a' in amazing—begins on the third beat of the bar and the 'maze' in "amazing" lands on the down-beat (as the groovy kids like to call it.) The first note of the tune, once we focus on the actual melodic map (which is an entirely different layer of interpretation than rhythm) is actually the fifth note in the major diatonic, seven note scale. Again, the 'maze' in "amazing" lands soundly on the first tone of that same scale. The interval between the first two notes is a perfect fifth.

Now at this point in my dissertation you may be puzzled. But I can assure you based on both my musical schooling and knowledge of the English language that everything I am telling you about "Amazing Grace" is the absolute truth. There's only one problem. I have yet to unwrap any of the deeper layers of understanding that have the potential to revolutionize how you view the song "Amazing Grace."

What about meaning? What about purpose?
What was it that inspired John Newton to write "Amazing Grace?" I could suggest the analysis you've been exposed to up to this point is faulty and even dangerous to your understanding of this hymn. But to do so would be robbing you of the opportunity to understand layers of this song that you may have never considered before. After all, English composition is a lifelong pursuit in its own right, while music notation and songwriting have led untold numbers of otherwise career-driven students away from promising careers in accounting and psychology into a fulfilling life of busking.

A skeptic, on the other hand, would take the opposite position, maintaining that questions of meaning and purpose are irrelevant, and that only the evidence available to our physical senses (phonetic, lyrical, rhythmic and musical) is worthy of our consideration. A musical agnostic—someone who claims that we can't know how a song comes to be—might suggest that the detailed analysis given above eliminates any need for contemplating the ultimate meaning (or cause) behind John Newton's creation. And our cynical friend would even welcome a debate as to why this tune needs to have an author at all. It is only a matter of time, says the musical agnostic, before letters (articulated without the existence of any phonetic code) began landing on the page, and eventually, given enough time and chance, form coherent phrases, and a few of those phrases happen to irk out a rustic rhyme scheme, which when uttered in a series of tones just happen to appeal to the auditory senses of an unknown audience who become so enamored with the unexpected 'tune' that they formalize its structure and repeat it whenever they feel the emotional urge to do so.

You mean a hit song? Yes. Or an idea that hints at something so much deeper than the mechanical structure that holds it together.

Of course, there are very few, if any, musical agnostics among us. No rational person would suggest that "Amazing Grace" happened without the assistance and inspiration of an inspired songwriter.

It would also be ridiculous if I tried to claim that the theological interpretation of "Amazing Grace" PROVES that the phonetic code, rhyme scheme, rhythm and melody are faulty or misleading descriptions. All of the descriptions as outlined above are accurate. And yet they are vastly different ways of coming to terms with all that is true about "Amazing Grace." I need all the layers to appreciate everything that the creator of this piece of music accomplished when he set out to tell his story. Not a single true statement about any one of the descriptive layers makes any of the other layers any less true.

As a fellow believer with John Newton in the amazing grace of God, I have discovered another layer, a higher level of meaning that is every bit as true as the music and lyrics. Higher in the sense that the purpose of the song occupies a much higher sphere of understanding than some of the mechanistic underlying layers. The characters, pulled from the twenty-six letters of the alphabet and used to compose the lyrics of "Amazing Grace," are a lot like DNA. I am able to understand the patterns and the relative meaning that those patterns convey. The words, phrases and rhyme schemes are a little like molecules or cellular structures. The greater our understanding of vocabulary and literary devices, the more I can identify what the author was trying to communicate. The melody of the song speaks a different language again, and my emotional and physiological response indicates that I have connected with the emotions of the songwriter.

But the meaning of the song, the reason for its existence, will never be discovered by describing it only in those terms.

47

A WALK IN THE PARK – PART 4

had spent almost seven hours in the Royal Tyrell Museum wandering from one exhibit hall to the next, trailing and sidestepping families on Sunday outings and dozens of curious tourists. Abandoned strollers and shrieking toddlers littered my path as I wandered in wonderment through several geologic ages. I retraced my steps on several occasions when I couldn't remember the name of a particular prehistoric creature or geologic formation that had caught my attention only moments before. I hadn't spoken to anyone in hours.

Brain weary, saturated with new terms, species and images, secure in the knowledge that trilobites were not an alien life form from some sci-fi movie I had failed to watch as a child, I headed for the parking lot.

After stealing one last glance at the badlands from above the museum, I climbed into my car and drove contentedly away from the Royal Tyrrell. The windows were up and the radio would stay off for the time being. Silence seemed the only appropriate response to the majestic drama that had played out before me over the last forty hours. Conversations with Marie at the dinosaur dig site yesterday mingled with the info-graphics of ancient life forms in the Burgess Shale exhibit on the second floor of the

Royall Tyrell. That montage gave way to images of the ominous thunderhead that had rolled eastward, invading the deserted coulees of Dinosaur Provincial Park last night, pinning me behind the tripod of my Nikon. I replayed my close inspection of a centrosaurine skeleton earlier in the day. I focused on the forearm structure. Was it only yesterday that I had crouched in the dirt 125 miles southwest of here and gently extracted an ulna fossil from its resting place? I had no energy to process any more data today, or for another month. After almost three years on the slippery slope, I had an odd feeling of restfulness. My journey was all but complete.

As I pulled out of the museum parking lot, the Red Deer River Valley appeared on my right. I was about to hit the gas and head for the Calgary Airport, but instead slowed and pulled over to the side of the road. This adventure wouldn't be complete until I had dipped my feet in the Red Deer River, the same river that had given life to the dreams of the dinosaur hunters over the past century. It had only been forty hours, give or take a couple of short nights in a musty hotel room, and yet I felt intimately connected to the brotherhood of paleontologists—all those who spend their lives scraping and digging in the earth, piecing together the past one fossil at a time. I left my rental at a rest stop and walked towards a stand of poplars decked out in summer greens and autumn yellow. The north bank of the river was a couple hundred yards off. In less than five minutes, I stood surveying the shallows, running shoes and socks piled behind me on a grassy ledge.

Carefully, I stepped over smooth river stones, away from the sandy bank. My aching feet cooled under the flow. I took another step. And another. I was now up to my knees.

I stood still, listening to the icy gurgle and the fall breeze in the poplars. And then I heard something else.

"Just your feet?"

It was a voice. Not audible, but unmistakable. It never crossed my mind to turn around and look for a human source. I knew who was speaking.

I contemplated the notion. Not so long ago I had began hiking the most unusual of paths only to come to the startling realization that my faith was mired in contempt for science, unable even to admit the presence of stifling sedimentary build-up. After questioning and reasoning, doing everything in my power to learn and unlearn some things, I had stumbled, and watched in painful disbelief as a faith system nurtured over a lifetime of evangelical fervor collapsed in on itself like a child's sandcastle at high tide. That had been the low point, but not the end.

"Just your feet?"

I stood silently, reliving the evidence as it played out in my mind. Some was as obvious as the centrosaurine vertebra that I had held in my hands only yesterday, some elusive, like the instructions for life coiled inside a double-helix strand of DNA. Some of the evidence still lies hidden, buried under compounding, error-riddled layers of fallible biblical interpretation.

"Just your feet?"

There's a sacrament in the Christian Church called baptism. In Evangelical circles we refer to it as believer's baptism. When a person wants to signify their intention to follow the way of Jesus, they do what he did. They get baptized in a tank at some church, or a swimming pool at a youth group barbeque. Or in a river. I had been a Christian for most of my life and had been baptized at our church by my father when I was a teenager.

But that day, standing in the Red Deer River, six hundred miles from the nearest gathering of family and encouraging onlookers, I was compelled to do it all again.

Carefully, I crouched down and scooped up stream water in my hands, held it aloft and poured it reverently on my head. For the next forty seconds I repeated this strange, sacred action as first my head, and then my shoulders, and eventually my entire body was soaked, symbolically cleansed in the pristine waters of the Red Deer River.

48
THE MIRACLE

As far as I know, God was my only witness that day as I bowed in the shallows of a lazy river in the badlands, washing away a lifetime of willful ignorance. I think they call it repentance.

Worship.

It was a simple, soggy act, a memorial to a faith that had died somewhere out on the slippery slope only to be reawakened by the fulfilled promise of resurrection and a renewed mind. In another place, another time, I might have referred to this recalibration of my theological compass as backsliding, but apart from those dozen dark days, I never felt like God was distancing himself from my relentless questions. And now, after all of this wandering and questioning and slipping sideways and getting back up again, I am at peace.

Perhaps it is possible that my attempt to squeeze faith and science, Genesis and Darwin, into a peaceable co-existence is not a fool's tale. Maybe looking into the natural world and Scripture together is ultimately the truest way of understanding our existence? How tragic it would be if my faith, or the faith of those around me, being propped up by a series of flimsy scientific trusses, was to crash down simply because I failed to search for and weigh the material evidence laid out before me? And how much more tragic it would be if a scientific theory opposed by so many because of a perceived threat to our faith was discovered to have some inherent properties that helped make even more sense of the Christian worldview?

What if evolution, as it was proposed by Darwin, really is, after all the yelling and legal wrangling, the way it actually happened. And if that is so then the story of how we arrived at this point in history is of vital importance, not simply so we can come to terms with our past, but because in our quest to make peace with our beginnings, followers of Christ can offer the story of God's intrusion into human history as an exclamation point to this incredible journey we call life.

To think that God, with only a word, released the laws of energy to run wild in the sands of an hourglass too vast to measure, while sustaining the building blocks of life with his own hands, orchestrating every turn in every strand of DNA in the early mists of time, while staring intently, gleefully, as creatures bearing unmistakable signs of his own personality emerged from the dust and shadows of creation. To think that this same God saw all of it and called his creation good.

That this God would then enter into the space–time dimension of my universe is a miracle. Not that he could, but that he would want to. The creator's enthusiasm for me is not diminished because my physical frame is simply dust. The DNA that has mapped the ascent of my physical frame is on an ancient, inspired trajectory, a holy pilgrimage that had its genesis in the lower life forms and continued upwards until the moment when God made his move, breathing something of his own spirit into my ancestors. *Homo sapiens*—no longer just an animal. Ever since that moment, we, as a race, have been learning what it means to communicate with each other and with our maker, and like every other lump of clay on the big cosmic wheel, we eventually discover that our purpose is, and always has been in the hands of the potter.

At my best, I am but a carbon-based life form on a trek to discover the divine, constantly waffling between good and evil, truth and deception, boxers and briefs. But in spite of my toxic self-centeredness, the creator, compelled to re-ignite a conversation that fell deathly silent before it had barely even begun in the mists of a garden long ago, chose to cross the space-time barrier and be born into the human family. Wholly divine—God—and yet wholly human.

Deity and dust intertwined. That is the miracle.

I am in wonder. I am stunned that the creator of the universe is inclined to love me, to come after me not in spite of, but because of, my evolutionary baggage.

He made me from dust to know him.

This is the story.

RESOURCE LIST

Books

Averbeck, Richard. *Reading Genesis 1-2: An Evangelical Conversation.*

Chapman, Matthew. *40 Days and 40 Nights: Darwin, Intelligent Design, God, Oxycontin, and Other Oddities on Trial in Pennsylvania.* New York: Collins, 2007.

Collins, Francis S. *The Language of God: A Scientist Presents Evidence for Belief.* New York: Free Press, 2006.

Coyne, Jerry A. *Why Evolution Is True.* New York: Penguin Group, 2009.

Dark, David. *The Sacredness of Questioning Everything.* Grand Rapids, Mich.: Zondervan, 2009.

Dawkins, Richard. *The Greatest Show on Earth: The Evidence for Evolution.* New York: Free Press, 2009.

Enns, Peter. *The Evolution of Adam: What the Bible Does and Doesn't Say about Human Origins.* Grand Rapids, MI: Brazos Press, 2012.

Garwood, Christine. *Flat Earth: The History of an Infamous Idea.* New York: Thomas Dunne Books, 2008.

Giberson, Karl. *Saving Darwin: How to Be a Christian and Believe in Evolution.* New York: HarperOne, 2008.

Henig, Robin Marantz. *The Monk in the Garden: The Lost and Found Genius of Gregor Mendel, the Father of Genetics.* Boston: Houghton Mifflin, 2000.

Miller, Kenneth R. *Finding Darwin's God: A Scientist's Search for Common Ground between God and Evolution.* New York: Cliff Street Books, 1999.

Miller, Kenneth R. *Only a Theory: Evolution and the Battle for America's Soul.* New York: Viking Penguin, 2008.

Nogar, Raymond J. *The Wisdom of Evolution.* Garden City, N.Y.: Doubleday, 1963.

Noll, Mark A. *The Scandal of the Evangelical Mind.* Grand Rapids, Mich.: W.B. Eerdmans, 1994.

Numbers, Ronald L. *The Creationists.* New York: A.A. Knopf :, 1992.

Parker, Andrew. *The Genesis Enigma: Why the Bible Is Scientifically Accurate.* New York: Dutton, 2009.

Polkinghorne, John C. *The Faith of a Physicist: Reflections of a Bottom-up Thinker.* New Jersey: Princeton University Press, 1994.

Quammen, David. *The Reluctant Mr. Darwin: An Intimate Portrait of Charles Darwin and the Making of His Theory of Evolution.* New York: Atlas Books/Norton, 2006.

Ryan, William B. F., and Walter C. Pitman. *Noah's Flood: The New Scientific Discoveries about the Event That Changed History.* New York: Simon & Schuster, 1998.

Schneiderman, Jill S. *For the Rock Record Geologists on Intelligent Design Creationism.* Berkeley: University of California Press, 2009.

Schroeder, Gerald L. *The Science of God: The Convergence of Scientific and Biblical Wisdom.* New York: Free Press, 1997.

Snoke, David. *A Biblical Case for an Old Earth.* Grand Rapids, Mich.: Baker Books, 2006.

Sobel, Dava. *Galileo's Daughter: A Historical Memoir of Science, Faith, and Love.* New York: Walker &, 1999.

Sykes, Bryan. *The Seven Daughters of Eve*. London: Bantam Press, 2001.

Vollmann, William T. *Uncentering the Earth: Copernicus and The Revolutions of the Heavenly Spheres*. New York: Norton, 2006.

Walton, John H. *The Lost World of Genesis One: Ancient Cosmology and the Origins Debate*. Downers Grove, Ill.: IVP Academic, 2009.

Witham, Larry. *The Measure of God: Our Century-long Struggle to Reconcile Science & Religion*. San Francisco: HarperSanFrancisco, 2005.

Other Sources (Papers, etc.)

Collins, Francis S. *Faith and the Human Genome*, from Perspectives on Science and Christian Faith

Collins, Francis S, *The Scientist as Believer*, Voices, February 2007, National Geographic Interactive, www.nationalgeographic.com/ngm/0702/voices.html

Coyne, Jerry: *The Faith That Dare Not Speak Its Name, The Case Against Intelligent Design*, taken from The New Republic, August 22 & 29, 2005

Davis A. Young, *A History of the Collapse of "Flood Geology" and a Young Earth* adapted from the book *The Biblical Flood: A Case Study of the Church's Response to Extrabiblical Evidence*, (Eerdmans, 1995)

Falk, Darrel R, *Coming To Peace With Science, Bridging the Worlds Between Faith and Biology*, Reading and Study Guide Companion

Galileo Galilei, Letter to Madame Christina of Lorraine, Grand Duchess of Tuscany: Concerning the Use of Biblical Quotations in Matters of Science (1615)[translation and footnotes by Stillman Drake, and confronted with the original Italian source *Lettera a Cristina di Lorena, Granduchessa di* Toscana, in *Opere* , edited by Antonio Favaro, Giunti-Barbera, Firenze 1968, vol. V, pp. 309-348]

Gingerich, Owen. *Did The Reformers Reject Copernicus?* from Christian History Institute, Issue 67, https://www.christianhistoryinstitute.org/magazine/article/did-the-reformers-reject-copernicus/

Keller, Tim K. *Creation, Evolution, and Christian Laypeople*, from The BioLogos Foundation, www.biologos.org/projects/scholar-essays

McGrath, Alister. *Augustine's Origin of Species, How the great theologian might weigh in on the Darwin debate.* | posted 5/08/2009 11:06AM

Miller, Keith B., *Theological Implications of an Evolving Creation* [This is a condensation of an article by the same title published in *Perspectives on Science and Christian Faith* 45, pp. 150-160 (1993).]

Newman, Robert C. *Evangelicals and Crackpot Science,* Interdisciplinary Biblical Research Institute Biblical Theological Seminary

West, John G. *Creationism And Intelligent Design Aren't The Same.* Research News and Opportunities in Science and Theology, December 1, 2002.

Van Der Plicht, Johannes. *Radiocarbon Dating and The Dead Sea Scrolls: A Comment on "Redating,"* Center for Isotope Research, Gronigen University and Faculty of Archaeology, Leiden University

Wright, N T. *How Can The Bible Be Authoritative?,* from Vox Evangelica 21, 1991

Young, Davis A. *The Contemporary Relevance of Augustine's View of Creation* Dept. of Geology, Geography & Environmental Studies   Calvin College Grand Rapids, Ml 49506
From: Perspectives on Science and Christian Faith 40.1:42-45 (3/1988)

An Armenian Perspective on the Search for Noah's Ark Presented at the 2007 Annual Meeting of the Near East Archaeological Society November 14-16, 2007 San Diego, California Richard D. Lanser, Jr., M.Div., Associates for Biblical Research

ABOUT THE AUTHOR

Calvin Wray was born in Victoria, British Columbia in 1963 and has lived in and around Vancouver all of his life. After graduating from the B.C. Institute of Technology in 1985 with an eye towards a career in architecture, he found himself heavily involved in several music projects and graphic design. As a freelance web designer and digital marketing specialist by day, Calvin now enjoys public speaking and engaging in lively discussions about the nature of faith and science. He lives in Surrey, B.C. with his family.

ACKNOWLEDGMENTS

Books don't write themselves and authors certainly don't think alone. Without the ongoing conversations that I have been privileged to take part in during the writing process, this story would not have landed in any manner resembling coherence. I'd like to thank everyone who listened, pushed back and dared me to dig deeper and explain myself better.

To Cory Alstad and Matthew Price, fellow creatives and two thirds of the Inklings 2.0, who sat and listened all those rainy nights as I tested my fledgling voice as a writer. Your friendship is highly valued.

To my wife Arlene, who supported me in this adventure, to Tessa and Tara, who never once rolled their eyes when I stepped onto my soapbox, your patience and interest in my journey kept me inspired.

To Dirk Buchner, my fellow heretic; thanks for listening and greasing the skids.

To David Sanford and Jim Hills, thank you for providing greatly needed professional expertise, editorial assistance and resources. Your advice kept me focused on what really matters.

To Randall and Kathy Jantzen, your passion in this project and your willingness to invest your energy and provide valuable feedback came at exactly the right time. Thank you for cheering me on.

To Elizabeth Jones, my long suffering editor; thanks for keeping space for me on your hard drive, while I hummed and hawed.

And to all of you who, by simply asking what I was up to and when I'd be finished, gave me the energy to push through: Robert Jantzen, Debbie and Denver Low, James Rowlinson, Rod Harris, Wendy Southam, Matt Bilton, Mike Newman, Roy Beugelink, Steve Faulkner, Vince Schofield, Joel Mayward, Dale and Anna Anaka, Sonja Stockle, Trevor Vellenoweth, Jean Howton, James Voth, Karel and Melissa Meyburg, Ken and Alison Redekop, Ron and Pearl Wiebe, Darryl and Shelley Cooper, Tim McCarthy, Joey Passi, Gord and Marie Kroegel, Kevin Southern, Rob Thiessen, Edgar and Barb Luck, and Sid Fensome. Your encouragement made all the difference.

And finally to Robert Longtin, who after meeting me for the first time, immediately stepped up to pay for a copy of my book. I still have that twenty with me as a reminder that ideas have value. I owe you much more than a book.

Made in the USA
Charleston, SC
22 October 2015